1545

|| Śrī Hari ||

Brave and Honest Children

Gita Press, Gorakhpur

[1545] 1 A

Seventh Reprint 2009 4,000
Total 33,000

❖ **Price : Rs. 15**
(Fifteen Rupees only)

ISBN 81-293-1091-0

Printed & Published by :
Gita Press, Gorakhpur—273005 (INDIA)
(a unit of Gobind Bhavan-Karyalaya, Kolkata)

Phone - (0551) 2334721, 2331250; Fax - (0551) 2336997
e-mail : **booksales@gitapress.org** website : **www.gitapress.org**

[1545]

Foreword

Bravery and honesty are the invaluable possessions of human life. They are part and parcel of a person's character and make his/her life successful and blissful.

This book consisting of 42 stories is the combined English version of the two Hindi story books **'Vīra Bālaka'** (Brave Boys) and **'Sacce Aura Īmānadāra Bālaka'** (True and Honest Children).

We hope that this book will prove immensely useful for our young generation in making them brave and honest. Children are requested to read these stories and draw inspiration from them.

—Publisher

CONTENTS

II Śrī Hari II

Brave Boys, Lava-Kuśa

The Supreme Person, Lord Śrī Rāma, in order to protect propriety, renounced His wife, Sītā, who was the topmost among the chaste wives. Lord Rāma and Sītā are inseparable. Both of them are one and the same. Their union and disunion is a pastime only. Lord Rāma did not renounce her in order to protect his name and fame or because of being defamed or out of harshness. He knew that Sītā was totally flawless. Her disunion afflicted Him very much. If in their disunion there was any harshness for Sītā, it was equally or even more for Lord Rāma. But Lord Rāma had incarnated Himself in order to establish righteousness in the world. If ideal persons are a bit lax in morals and conduct, other people are induced to commit deadly sins and crimes by pretending to follow their footsteps. Circumstances had forced Sītā to stay in Aśoka garden in Laṅkā, ruled by Rāvaṇa, as a captive. So some people began to doubt her chastity. Therefore Lord Rāma, in order to save the women and men from unchaste and immortal conduct, had to be terribly harsh to His own self. He also wanted to set an example for other rulers that they should be ever prepared to make the greatest personal sacrifice to set an example for the public.

Having obeyed Lord Rāma; Lakṣmaṇa being helpless, left Sītā in the forest near Vālmīki's hermitage when she was pregnant. Great Sage Vālmīki gave her protection in his hermitage and there she gave birth to twin brothers, Lava and Kuśa. Great Sage Vālmīki performed all ceremonies of the two boys and imparted them training in arms and missiles. Besides this, the great sage also taught them the recitation of 'Vālmīki Rāmāyaṇa'. When the two brothers recited the Rāmāyaṇa, having twenty-four thousand verses, seven sections and five hundred cantos, in a soft, melodious, musical tone, the audience was spell bound.

In Ayodhyā, Lord Rāma performed the 'Aśvamedha-sacrifice'. According to the scriptural ordinance, the black coloured horse was set free. Śatrughnajī with Prince Puṣkala and army-commander, Kālajit, having a big army started for the protection of the horse. Śrī Hanumān and Sugrīva, the king of monkeys, with the army of monkeys and bears, joined them. The horse was free to go in any direction of its own accord. The army followed the horse at a little distance so that the horse could not be put to any inconvenience. Several kings themselves paid tax to Śatrughnajī, some of the kings paid tax when they were pursued. In certain cases they had to battle. In this way the horse of the sacrifice, having got victory, wandering, reached the forest, near the sacred grove of the great sage Vālmīki.

At that time Lava was playing with other boys in the forest. Having seen the well adorned horse, ornamented with gold, studded with jewels, the boys came near the horse. A proclamation was written in clear and beautiful letters on a banner, which was tied on the head of the horse. It was written on it, "This horse is the sacrifice-horse of Lord Rāma, the emperor of a vast empire; and a great valiant warrior. Śatrughnajī is protecting it. The region by which this horse passes by, will be regarded as won by Śatrughnajī. If any Kṣatriya (member of the warrior class) has the courage not to accept the emperor of Ayodhyā as his emperor, he should catch the horse and battle." Having read this proclamation Lava was enraged. He tied the horse to a tree and holding a bow and an arrow stood to battle. First other boys (sages' sons) tried to persuade him not to indulge in battle, but when he did not agree, they stood at some distance to see the scene of the battle.

The guards, who were following the horse, saw that a boy had tied the horse to a tree. When they asked Lava, he said, "I have tied it. My brother, Kuśa shall be angry with the person who tries to untie it." The guards thought that he was talking in a childish manner, so they went ahead to untie it. When Lava saw that they were acting against his will, he cut off their arms by shooting arrows. The guards ran away and they conveyed the message to Śatrughnajī that the horse had been tied by a boy.

Having seen the arms of his soldiers cut off and having listened to the message, conveyed by the guards, Śatrughnajī understood that the boy was not ordinary. He ordered the commander to draw up the army in battle array. The entire army was arrayed properly in battle array so that no enemy could penetrate it. Then all of them went to the place where the horse was tied. The commander tried to bring the boy round by persuasion, when he saw a small boy prepared to shoot arrows. Lava said, "If you are afraid of the battle, return. I let you go. Tell Śrī Rāma, the owner of this horse that Lava has tied the horse." At last the battle was waged. When Lava showered arrows, a stampede in the army ensued. Elephants, horses and soldiers were killed. The commander Kālajit waged the battle valiantly but Lava made all his efforts vain and cut off both his arms and head.

First Śatrughnajī did not believe the news, conveyed by his soldiers that any one could kill his invincible commander. But finally listening to all the details, consulting the adviser, he himself with his army went to the battle-field. The big army surrounded Lava from all sides. When Lava saw that he was surrounded by the enemies, he began to scatter the soldiers with his arrows. When Puṣkala saw that the soldiers, being frightened, were fleeing, he went forward to fight. But Lava wounded him and he (Puṣkala) became unconscious in a short battle. Then Hanumānajī came forward to battle. He showered stones and trees on Lava but Lava cut them into pieces. Being enraged, Hanumānjī rolled him in his tail. Then Lava, thinking of his mother, gave a blow on his tail. With this blow, Hanumānjī was tormented due to the blow and he freed Lava. Then Lava made him unconscious with his arrows. Then Śatrughnajī himself came to fight. After a tough fight, Śatrughnajī also lost consciousness. When Śatrughnajī became unconscious, then kings such as Suratha etc., made a fierce attack on Lava. Lava all alone was fighting bravely against those great warriors. After sometime Śatrughna regained consciousness. Then he shot the arrow, offered to him by Lord Rāma, with which he had killed the demon,

Lavaṇāsura. When that radiant arrow struck Lava's chest, Lava fell down unconscious. Śatrughna was thinking to carry unconscious Lava to Ayodhyā in a chariot.

The sons of the sages who were witnessing this battle, came running to Sītājī in great sage Vālmīki's hermitage and conveyed the news, "Mother, your younger son tied the horse of a king. The soldiers fought against him and he has lost consciousness and they want to take him with them." Having heard this, mother Sītā was sad, her eyes filled with tears. In the meanwhile Kuśa came there and having known all the details, that his brother had lost consciousness, he was enraged. He prostrated at the feet of his mother and seeking permission from her, ran towards the battle-field with his bow and arrows.

Lava at that time was lying in the chariot and he had regained consciousness. Seeing his brother coming, he jumped from the chariot. Both the brothers began to shoot arrows and kill warriors—Kuśa from the east direction and Lava from the west direction. Both brothers filled the battle-field with dead bodies. Great warriors, by fleeing, tried to save their lives. Whosoever came, both of them wounded him badly with their arrows. Lava and Kuśa threw Hanumānjī and Aṅgada in the sky with their arrows again and again. When they began to fall on the earth, they would again toss them through the air. Thus they tossed them again and again like balls, and they suffered severe pain in their bodies, and when Lava and Kuśa out of grace stopped their arrows; both of them fell on the ground and lost consciousness. Kuśa also injured Śatrughnajī badly with his arrows and made him unconscious. The great warrior Suratha, being wounded by Kuśa's arrows, fell down on the ground and Kuśa ensnared Sugrīva in 'Varuṇa Pāśa' (sea-god noose). Thus Kuśa was victorious in the battle-field.*

When they had got victory, Lava said to Kuśa, "Brother! By your grace I could cross this ocean of battle. Now let us have some souvenir for this battle." Both the brothers first went to Śatrughnajī and extracted the precious jewel from his crown. Then Lava took Puṣkala's crown. Both the brothers also took the precious ornaments of their arms and also their weapons and missiles.

* In Śrī Rāmīya Aśvamedha Purāṇa it has been described that when Śatrughnajī became unconscious, the message was sent to Ayodhyā and then Lakṣmaṇa came with the army. When Lakṣmaṇa lost consciousness, Bharata and at last Lord Rāma came to the battle-field. Lord Rāma did not fight because He did not think it proper to fight against His own sons. So He slept in the chariot. Lava and Kuśa thought that He had become unconscious because an arrow struck Him.

Then Lava said, "Dear brother, I'll also take these two monkeys with me. After seeing them, our mother will laugh and other boys will be pleased and it will be a source of entertainment for them." So each of them caught the tail of Sugrīva and Hanumān respectively and went towards the hermitage.

Having seen her sons coming, Sītā was very much pleased, because she was waiting for their safe return. When she saw her sons coming, catching the tails of two monkeys, there was smile on her face; but when she recognized the monkeys, she said, "Why have you caught them. Free them quickly. One of them is brave Hanumān who burnt Laṅkā to ashes and the second is Sugrīva, the king of monkeys. Why have you disregarded them?"

Lava and Kuśa, with a simple heart, narrated the reason of the battle and its result. Then Sītā said, "Sons, you have done an unjust act. That is your father's horse. Free the horse and also free these monkeys."

Then Lava and Kuśa said, "Dear mother, we tied the horse by discharging our duty as Kṣatriyas (members of warrior class). The great sage Vālmīki had taught us that a Kṣatriya, who fights in a battle with righteousness, does not incur sin. Now by your order we are going to free these monkeys and the horse as well."

Sītājī had a resolve, "If even mentally, besides Lord Rāma, I have never thought of any other person; and if I have ever followed the path of righteousness strictly, let all the wounded, unconscious and dead warriors in the battle be alive and healthy."

As soon as she made this utterance, all the warriors came back to life, as if they had waked from sleep. Their limbs, which had been cut off, were joined and there was no mark of injury on their bodies. Śatrughnajī saw that there was no jewel in his crown. Puṣkala had lost his crown, ornaments, weapons and missiles. Their horse was standing before them. They went back to Ayodhyā with the horse and narrated the whole incident to Lord Rāma.

When the horse came back to Ayodhyā, the religious sacrifice was started. Sages with their disciples came there from afar. The great sage, Vālmīki also with Lava, Kuśa and other disciples came and stayed on the bank of the Sarayū, at a little distance from the city. With the order of the great sage, Lava and Kuśa went about reciting the Rāmāyaṇa in the hermitages of sages, in the camps of the kings and in the streets of the city. People assembled to listen to their clear, sweet and musical

recitation. All around there was a talk of the recitation of the two brothers. One day Lord Rāma with Bharata also listened to their recitation from the roof of their palace. Both Lava and Kuśa, with due reverence, were called to the palace and were requested to recite the Rāmāyaṇa. Lord Rāma wanted to give them eighteen thousand guineas as a prize but Lava and Kuśa did not accept this offer. As Lava and Kuśa suggested, when there was no sacrifice, that time was fixed for the recitation of the Rāmāyaṇa. At that time the public, the invited kings, sages and monkeys etc., listened to their wonderful recitation of the Rāmāyaṇa. When the full biography of Lord Rāma was recited, all the people came to know that both the boys were Sītā's sons.

The Supreme Person Lord Rāma called Sītājī to prove her chastity by taking an oath in the assembly before all the people. Sītā, the mother of the world came and taking on oath said, "If I am totally pious, the earth may absorb me, within it." The earth burst with a tumult. The earth revealed itself as a goddess with a throne and asked Sītā to sit on it and disappeared. The surface of the earth became flat. Now nothing else remains to be said. Lava and Kuśa could not receive the love of their father since their birth and when they met their father, they lost their dear mother. How could they become happy by becoming princes?

Brave Prince, Kuvalayāśva

One day the great sage, Gālava came to the valiant King, Śatrujit. The great sage also brought a divine horse with him. The king adored him in accordance with the scriptural ordinance. The great sage said to the king, "A wicked demon with his debiding (demoniac) potency, having assumed the forms of a lion or a tiger or an elephant and such other wild animals, comes to the hermitage and destroys it. Though he can be burnt to ashes out of anger, yet by doing so, the penance will bear no fruit. So we don't want our penance to go in vain. Having seen our sufferings, the sun-god has sent this horse, 'Kuvalaya' to us. This horse can go round the entire earth without getting tired and it can go to the celestial world, nether world and can move on the water. The deities have said that your son Ṛtadhvaja, riding this horse, will kill this demon. So kindly, send the prince with us. Having got this horse, he will be known in the world as 'Kuvalayāśva'.

Having obeyed the great sage, the righteous king ordered the prince to go with the great sage. The prince went with the great sage and began to live in his hermitage. One day when the sages were offering evening prayers, the mean demon, assuming the form of a pig, reached there in order to oppress the sages. Having seen him, the disciples of the sages made a noise. The Prince Ṛtadhvaja, riding the horse, chased him. He, having pulled his bow, pierced the demon with a crescent shaped arrow. Being wounded with the arrow, the demon ran to save his life. The prince, riding the horse, chased him through forests, mountains and bushes, wherever the demon went. At last the demon, running very fast, jumped into a pit. The prince also with his horse jumped into that pit. That was the way leading to the nether

world. By that dark path, the prince reached the nether world. Having reached the nether world, which was as beautiful as the heaven, he tied the horse and went to a palace. There he met the daughter of Viśvāvasu, the king of Gandharvas (celestial singers and musicians). The wicked son, Pātālaketu, of the demon, Vrajaketu had abducted her from heaven and brought her to the nether world. That demon wanted to marry her. When Madālasā came to know that the prince had pierced the demon, Pātālaketu with his arrow, she accepted Ṛtadhvaja as her husband.

When the prince had married Madālasā, Pātālaketu came to know this news and he, being enraged, came there with his follower-demons. The demons showered weapons and missiles on the prince but the prince, while smiling, cut those weapons and missiles with his arrows. He, having used the divine weapon, Tvāṣṭra, killed all the demons in a moment. As the great sage Kapila's fire of anger burnt sixty thousand sons of Sagara to ashes, likewise the fire of that divine weapon burnt the demons to ashes.

The prince with his wife, riding the horse, left the nether world and went to his house. Having seen his victorious son, his father was very much pleased with him. Afterwards the prince Ṛtadhvaja became king Kuvalayāśva. His wife Madālasā knew the Supreme-Reality. It was she who, while lullabying her sons, imparted them the knowledge of the Supreme.

Brave Demon-boy, Barbarīka

Bhīmasena, a valiant warrior, the son of Pāṇḍu married Hiḍimbā, a demon-woman. She gave birth to a very brave son, Ghaṭotkaca. He, having obeyed Lord Kṛṣṇa, married a very beautiful lady named Kāmakaṭaṅkatā, the daughter of the demon, Mura. She gave birth to Barbarīka. The sons of female demons become young and strong as soon as they are born. The boy Barbarīka had been polite, righteous and brave since birth. He with his father Ghaṭotkaca went to Dvārakā and both of them bowed to Lord Kṛṣṇa. Barbarīka with folded hands prayed to Lord Kṛṣṇa, "O Primal Lord! I bow down to You by concentrating my mind, thinking faculty (Citta) and intellect. O Supreme Person! How does a being attain salvation? Different people have different opinions about the highest goal of life—such as charity, austerity, wealth, pleasures and salvation. O Lord! Out of these preach me the gospel, which is conducive to the highest goal for my family."

The Lord said, "O son, a man can attain the highest goal of his life by acting according to the family and Varṇa (caste) [order of life] in which he is born. To a Brāhmaṇa (priest) austerity, control over senses and study of the scriptures lead to the highest goal. For a Kṣatriya (member of the warrior class) the first and foremost quality is strength (power) because by using his power, he destroys the wicked and protects the good and it leads him to the supreme goal (benediction). A Vaiśya, by rearing animals, by farming and by trade earns wealth and then by offering charity becomes eligible to attain the highest goal. A Śūdra (member of the labour class) becomes eligible for salvation (benediction) by serving the members of the three social orders. You are born in a Kṣatriya family, therefore you should muster incomparable power. Power is mustered by the grace of Durgā, the goddess of power, therefore you should worship the goddesses of power."

When Barbarīka asked Lord Kṛṣṇa, He said to him to go to the place of pilgrimage named Mahīsāgara-Saṅgama and there he should worship the nine goddesses of power. He worshipped for three years and then the goddesses, being pleased with him, appeared before him and granted him the boon that he would be endowed with very rare incomparable power in the three worlds. Then the goddesses said to him, "Son, reside here for sometime. Here a Brāhmaṇa (member of the priest class) named Vijaya will come and with his association you will be endowed with more power."

Having obeyed the goddesses, Barbarīka began to reside there. After some days, the Brāhmaṇa, Vijaya from Magadha country came there. He worshipped Lord Śiva in His seven forms such as Kumāreśvara etc., and also worshipped goddesses for many days. The goddesses in his dream ordered him, "You, worship the goddess of perfection in the courtyard of her temple—Our devotee, Barbarīka will help you."

Vijaya next morning said to Barbarīka, the grandson of Bhīma, "Recite the hymn of the goddess, being pious and free from sleep so that till I continue my worship no one may create an obstacle."

Vijaya, having concentrated his mind, began to worship the goddess and Barbarīka being alert, stood up, protecting Vijaya so that none could get in the way of his worship. He killed the demon, Repalendra and female demon Druhadruhā who tried to disturb him in his worship. After that he went to the nether world and killed the terrible demons 'Palāsī' who tortured 'Nāgas'.

When those demons were killed; Vāsuki, the king of Nāgas (snakes) praised Barbarīka and being pleased with him told him to ask for a boon. Barbarīka said "Let Vijaya attain perfection, without any obstacle, by worship."

When he was going out of the nether world, very beautiful girls of Nāga clan, being fascinated by his appearance and bravery, requested him to marry them; but self-controlled Barbarīka did not accept their request because he had taken a vow to remain a celibate for ever.

When Barbarīka returned from the nether world, Vijaya embraced him. That perfected soul said, "I have attained perfection by your grace. There is very pious vermilion coloured ash in the vessel for offering oblation, take a handful of it. If you leave this ash in the battle-field, even death will not get victory over you, death itself will die. Thus you will easily get victory over your enemies."

Barbarīka said, "A noble man is he who does good to others without any selfish motive. Can a man, who does good to others, for getting a reward, be noble? Please, give this ash to anyone else. I am happy, seeing you successful and happy."

The deities offered 'Siddhi' (perfection) to Vijaya. So he was named 'Siddhasena'. He left that place. After sometime the Pāṇḍavas, having been defeated in gambling, wandering through forests and in the places of pilgrimage, reached that place of pilgrimage. The five Pāṇḍavas and Draupadī were very much tired. After having a vision of the goddess 'Caṇḍikā', they sat there. Barbarīka was also sitting there. But neither the Pāṇḍavas had seen Barbarīka, nor Barbarīka had seen the Pāṇḍavas. So they could not recognize each other. When thirsty Bhīmasena began to go into the pond to drink water, Yudhiṣṭhira said to him, "First wash your hands and feet at some distance from this pond, by taking water and then drink water." But Bhīmasena was feeling restless out of thirst. So without paying attention to what Yudhiṣṭhira said, he went into the pond and began to wash his hands and feet there. Having seen him doing so, Barbarīka said, scolding him, "You are polluting the pond of the goddess by washing your hands and feet in it. I always give a bath to the goddess with this water. When you have not even so much of sense, why do you go on pilgrimage in vain?"

Bhīmasena, roaringly, scolded Barbarīka and said, "Water is to take bath; and bath in the place of pilgrimage is sanctioned by the scriptures." Thus he supported his action. But Barbarīka said, "At the place of pilgrimage where there is flowing water, bath can be taken inside the river or stream etc. But as far as a well or a pond is concerned, the scriptural ordinance is to take water from it and to bathe outside it. First hands and feet should be washed in the water of the pond—from which water to give bath to the deities is not taken, and that should be at some distance from the temple of the goddess. Those who throw rubbish, waste matter, urine, phlegm, spit and also water from the mouth into water are like murderers of Brāhmaṇas (members of the priest class).

He, whose hands, feet, mind and senses are under control and who is self-restrained, gets the fruit of pilgrimage. It is better to live a short life by performing virtuous actions than to live a very long life by doing sinful deeds. Therefore come out of this tank very quickly."

When Bhīmasena paid no heed to Barbarīka's advice, which was ordained by the scriptures, then Barbarīka began to throw pebbles on Bhīmasena's forehead. Bhīmasena immediately came out and began to fight with Barbarīka. Both of them were very valiant. So both of them began to wrestle. After sometime Bhīmasena lost vigour and zeal. Barbarīka raised Bhīmasena up and wanted to throw him into the sea. When he reached the seashore with Bhīmasena in his hands, Lord Śiva, standing in the air said, "O noble demon, free him from your clutches, he is your grandfather, Bhīmasena, son of Pāṇḍu, he deserves reverence from you."

When Barbarīka heard these words, he freed Bhīmasena and prostrated at his feet. He reproached himself, wept bitterly and craved forgiveness. Having seen him very restless, Bhīmasena embraced him and said, "Dear son, you are not at fault. It was my mistake. A Kṣatriya must punish the wrong doer. I am very much pleased with you. My ancestors are blessed that in their family such a righteous son is born. You are to be praised by virtuous men. You should not grieve."

Barbarīka did not get rid of his grief. He said to Bhīmasena, "O grandfather! I don't deserve to be praised. There is penitence for all sinful acts, but he, who is not devoted to parents, does not attain salvation. I'll leave this body by jumping into the 'Mahīsāgara-Saṅgama' (ocean) so that I may not commit such a sin in other lives."

He reached the shore of the ocean and was ready to jump into it. At that time the Goddess Ambikā, with four goddesses of the four directions, with Lord Śiva appeared there. They stopped Barbarīka from committing suicide. So, being sad, he came back. The Pāṇḍavas were wonderstruck and pleased with his bravery.

When Pāṇḍavas' period of exile ended and the evil souled Duryodhana refused to return their kingdom, then preparations for the war in the holy field of Kurukṣetra began. At the beginning of the war, Yudhiṣṭhira put a question to Arjuna about the bravery of the great warriors of his army. Having praised the bravery of all the great warrior of his army, at last he said, "I am capable to destroy the entire Kaurava army in a day." Having heard his word, Barbarīka could not help speaking. He said, "I have such divine weapons, missiles and other materials that I can send the entire Kaurava army to the abode of the god of death in 48 minutes."

Lord Kṛṣṇa supported Barbarīka statement and then asked, "Dear son! How can you kill the Kaurava army, protected by Bhīṣma and Droṇa etc., in 48 minutes?"

Having heard Lord Kṛṣṇa's question, incomparable and valiant Barbarīka shot a hollow arrow filling it with red colour. The ash flying

with his arrow fell on the vital spots of the warriors of the two armies. It did not fall on the bodies of Pāṇḍavas, Kṛpācārya and Aśvatthāmā. Having done so, Barbarīka said, "You have seen that I have examined the vital spots of the warriors who will be killed. Now I shall kill them by striking the vital spots with the sharp arrows, offered to me by the goddess. I request you to take an oath in the name of righteousness, not to wield any weapon. I am going to kill enemies in 48 minutes."

Barbarīka was very valiant, righteous and also humble but at that time, out of egoism, he transgressed the limits of ethical propriety. The gods and sages had granted boons to several warriors of both the armies. If all the boons had proved vain, the propriety of gods, righteousness and penance would have been destroyed. Lord Kṛṣṇa, Who had incarnated Himself for the protection of the ethical propriety, having heard Barbarīka's statement, cut down his head with His discus.

At Barbarīka's death, all the people were stunned. The Pāṇḍavas were grief-stricken. Ghaṭotkaca fell down unconscious. At that time fourteen goddesses appeared. They explained to Ghaṭotkaca and the Pāṇḍavas that Barbarīka in his previous birth was a gnome, named Sūryavarcā. When the deities with Brahmājī were offering praises to Lord Viṣṇu on the Meru Mountain and praying to Him to rid the earth of unrighteousness and the wicked, then out of egoism, that gnome said that he would rid the earth of unrighteousness. It was because of his pride that Brahmājī, being displeased with him, called down curse upon him that when the Lord manifested Himself to rid the rid of unrighteousness, He would kill him. In order to prove that curse true, Lord Kṛṣṇa has killed Barbarīka.

As was ordered by the Lord, the goddesses by applying nectar, made the head of Barbarīka ever young and immortal. The head expressed desire to witness the scene of the war. Therefore the Lord established this head on a mountain and granted the boon to it that it would be worshipped in the world.

At the end of the Mahābhārata war, Yudhiṣṭhira was expressing his gratitude to Lord Kṛṣṇa again and again that it was by His grace that they could get victory. Bhīmasena thought that it was he who had killed the sons of Dhṛtarāṣṭra, then why Yudhiṣṭhira was praising Lord Kṛṣṇa so much. When Bhīmasena said so, Arjuna wanted to make it clear to him that ever victorious valiant warriors such as Bhīṣma and Droṇa were not killed by him and they were merely instruments. They got victory owing to an unknown person whom he ever saw ahead of him on the war front.

Having listened to Arjuna's utterance, Bhīmasena burst into laughter and he thought that Arjuna was under an illusion. In order to come to the right conclusion, he with Arjuna and Lord Kṛṣṇa went to the mountain and asked Barbarīka's head, "O dear son, you have witnessed the entire scene of the war. Tell us who has killed the Kauravas in the war?"

Barbarīka said, "I have seen only one person fighting against the enemies. He had five heads and ten hands on his left hand side, in which he was wielding weapons such as trident etc. On his right hand side, he had one head and four hands in which he was holding weapons and missiles such as discus etc. On his left hand side he had tresses and on his forehead the moon was shining, his limbs were smeared with ashes. On the right hand side, the crown was sparkling with brilliance, the limbs were besmeared with sandalwood paste and round the neck the Kaustubha jewel was dazzling. I have not seen any other person besides him, killing the warriors of the Kaurava army."

When Barbarīka said so, the flowers were showered from the sky. Bhīmasena, being ashamed, craved forgiveness. Lord Kṛṣṇa forgave him because He is the ocean of mercy. He, smilingly, embraced Bhīmasena.

The Lord went to Barbarīka's head and said "You should not leave this area."

Brave Boy, Abhimanyu

The Mahābhārata war was being waged. Grand father, Bhīṣma was lying on the bed of arrows and the preceptor, Droṇa had become the commander of the Kaurava army. Duryodhana time and again said to the preceptor, "You are partial to the Pāṇḍavas. If you don't favour them, it is very easy for you to get victory over them." The preceptor, being excited, said, "So long as Arjuna is on the war front, even the gods cannot get victory over the Pāṇḍava army. If you remove Arjuna from the war front, I'll defeat the remaining army." Being instigated by Duryodhana, the brave warriors named Saṁśaptaka challenged Arjuna to fight with them and they carried him away to fight, far from the war front. On the war front the preceptor, Droṇa drew up his army in battle-array in the form of a circle. When Yudhiṣṭhira came to know this fact, he was very much disappointed and sad. In the Pāṇḍavas army only Arjuna knew how to pierce (cross) the battle-array. In the absence of Arjuna, Pāṇḍavas defeat seemed to be certain. When Abhimanyu, the fifteen year old son of Arjuna and Subhadrā perceived Yudhiṣṭhira and other warriors of his side, getting disappointed, he said, "Sire, don't worry, I'll enter (cross) the battle-array and remove conceit (vanity) of the hostile army."

Yudhiṣṭhira asked, "O Son! How do you know the secret of the battle-array in the form of a circle?"

Abhimanyu said, "I was in the womb of my mother. Then one day my father described the battle-array to my mother. My father explained to cross the six gates (ways) of the battle-array, in the meanwhile my mother fell asleep. The father did not explain it further. Therefore, I entering the battle-array, can cross the six gates but I don't know how to cross the seventh gate and come back out."

Bhīmasena said full of enthusiasm, "I'll break the seventh gate with my club." Though Yudhiṣṭhira did not want to send Abhimanyu to the battle-array, but there was no alternative. Abhimanyu was a mighty chariot warrior and took part in the war as a warrior daily. He insisted to pierce the battle-array. Next day the war started and the responsibility to protect the main gate of the battle-array in the form of a circle, was shouldered by Jayadratha, husband of Duryodhana's sister. When Jayadratha undertook austere penance, Lord Śiva granted him the boon, that except Arjuna, he would get victory over other Pāṇḍavas. Abhimanyu showered arrows in such a manner that Jayadratha lost courage and Abhimanyu could pierce the battle-array. But soon Jayadratha regained courage and stood at the gate of the battle-array, being alert. In spite of making best of efforts throughout the day, Bhīmasena or any other warrior could not enter the battle-array. Only Jayadratha could check them all because of the boon granted to him.

Fifteen year old Abhimanyu, sitting in his chariot, entered the battle-array of the enemy. Weapons and missiles were being showered on him from the four quarters but he was not afraid in the least. He also showered arrows on all sides. Elephants, horses and warriors of the Kaurava army were slaughtered. The chariots were broken to pieces. There was cry of distress all around. The warriors fled here and there. Great warrior such as Droṇa, Karṇa, Aśvatthāmā, Śalya etc., came to face him but no one could defeat him. He cut off the divine weapons of the enemies with the divine weapons. Even great warriors such as Droṇa and Karṇa could not face him. He made such a push that they had to retrogress time and again. He, having defeated the great warrior guards, who safe-guarded the gates of the battle-array, marched forward. He pierced six gates.

Abhimanyu was all alone and he had to wage war continuously. The great chariot warriors whom he had already defeated, again came there and surrounded him. He did not know the vital spot of the seventh entrance. In spite of all the adverse circumstances, he neither felt fatigued nor his zeal slackened. On the other hand great chariot warriors of the Kaurava army had been wounded by him with his arrows. Droṇa plainly declared—'So long as this boy wields the bow, we should not expect to get victory over him."

Six great chariot warriors jointly attached Abhimanyu by foul means. Four of them killed one horse of his chariot each. One of them killed his chariot driver and Karṇa cut his bow into pieces. In spite of all these adverse circumstances, Abhimanyu jumped from his chariot and attacked the hostile army. Once again a stampede ensued. Cruel enemies had unjustly surrounded him from all sides. All of them attacked him at a time. His armour and helmet had been cut and they had fallen down. With arrows he was badly wounded and blood was flowing from his body. When his weapons were cut, he attacked with the wheel of the chariot. Even then no one could defeat him. The enemies struck his naked head, without helmet with a club from the back side. Abhimanyu fell down on the battle-field and met a heroic end. Therefore Lord Kṛṣṇa, consoling his sister, Subhadrā, declared that such a heroic death is desirable for all, including Himself.

Brave Boy, Bharata

Ṛṣabhadeva's son, Bharata was self-disciplined, dispassionate and wise while Duṣyanta's son Bharata was brave and heroic. Our country is named 'Bhārata' because of these two noble souls and this country glorifies dispassion, wisdom, bravery and heroism. Ṛṣabha's son, Bharata, became a royal sage. Duṣyanta's son Bharata was very brave and heroic in his boyhood. He was born in a hermitage and the name of his mother was Śakuntalā who brought him up. When he was only a child, he crawled and reached near a lion or a tiger and began to pat its face with his palm. When he learnt to walk, he caught cubs and he was not afraid at all, when they growled. He said to a lion, "I'll count the number of your teeth." Then he put his hand into the lion's mouth and counted the teeth. When he was only four years old, he pulled the ear of the tiger and then sat on its back

by clapping. He showed a stick to the lion and the tiger and addressed them, "Sit down, I'll not hit you. Wrestle with me and I'll throw you down, I'll not be defeated." The lion, and the tiger moved their tails by expressing their love. Elephants and bears brought sweet fruits and offered those fruits to him. His mother always was pleased with such a fearless son and she declared that her son would be a great and successful ruler. At last Bharata became a great and righteous king. The brave people sing his heroic and glorious deeds even today.

Brave Boy, Skandagupta

Hūṇas and Śakas etc., living in the deserted area of middle Asia, are the barbarian tribes, which lived there in the fifth century. The people of these tribes were militant warriors and cruel. They attacked Europe several times and desolated it. A great Rome empire was destroyed by their attacks. They also robbed China several times. There was a cry of distress in the country which they attacked.

Once the news was received that a big army of Hūṇas had assembled on the other side of the Himālaya to attack Bhārata (India). At that time in Bhārata (India) Magadha was the biggest state. The king of that state was Kumāragupta. His son, prince Skandagupta was not yet a youth. As soon as the news of the assembly of the Hūṇa army was received, Skandagupta, running, went to his father. At that time the king was consulting his ministers and commanders to wage war against the Hūṇas. Skandagupta said to his father, "I will also go to the war front to wage the war."

The king, Kumāragupta explained to his son, "Hūṇas are very valiant and cruel. They wage an unrighteous war and their number is also large. To wage the war against them is an invitation to death."

But the prince, Skandagupta was not terrified. He said, "Dear father, it is a very auspicious occasion for a Kṣatriya (member of the warrior class), if he dies in order to protect his country and righteousness. I will fight death and save my country from the attack of the cruel enemies." King Kumāragupta embraced his brave son and consented him to go to the war front accompanied by two lac brave soldiers. Those brave soldiers started from Patna and crossing Punjab, climbed the snow covered peaks of the Himālaya. They marched forward facing the terrible cold, cold wave and snow-storm.

Hūṇas could never think that any one could attack them. When they saw that a big army was coming to attack them from the peak of the Himālaya, they also got ready to wage the war. They were wonderstruck to see that a small boy, riding the horse with a naked sword, blowing the conch, was leading the army. He was Prince Skandagupta.

The war began. Prince Skandagupta slaughtered so many enemies that the war front was filled with dead bodies. After a short time Hūṇas lost heart and a stampede ensued in the Hūṇa army. When Skandagupta, having got victory over the enemy, crossing the Himālaya, came to his country, lacs of people had already assembled to give an enthusiastic welcome to him. From the capital, Magadha, upto a distance of ten miles, the path was decorated. The whole country celebrated a festival to give a warm welcome to him.

Prince Skandagupta afterwards became the emperor of Bhārata. He had extended his empire upto the areas which are called Iran and Afghanistan today. It is difficult to find such a valiant warrior in the history of any other country besides India. He, having conquered the world, performed the 'Aśvamedha sacrifice' in which the horse was set free. Besides being valiant, he was a very righteous, generous and just emperor.

Brave Boy, Caṇḍa

At that time Rāṇā Lākhā ruled over Chittaur. He was so valiant that he had defeated Lodī, the king of Delhi. His fame spread far and wide. Among his sons, Caṇḍa was the eldest and most virtuous. The king of Jodhpur sent a coconut (a proposal) to marry his daughter to the prince of Chittaur. When the Brāhmaṇa (a member of the priest class) reached the royal court, the prince, Caṇḍa was not there. When the Brāhmaṇa said that he had brought the coconut (an emblem of marriage proposal) for the prince, Rāṇā Lākhā, humorously, said—'I thought that you have brought this coconut for this old man and you want to play a game with me." Having heard this, all the people laughed.

At that time the prince, Caṇḍa was coming to the court. He had heard what his father had said. So he very politely said, "It may be out of humour, but when my father said that the coconut was sent for him, it means that she has become my mother. So I can't marry her."

Now it was a very serious matter. If the coconut was sent back, it was an insult to the king of Jodhpur as well as to his innocent daughter; and the prince, Caṇḍa was not at all prepared to marry her. His father did his best to persuade him, but he did not budge an inch. When the king saw his obedient son to be insistent, he was enraged. He angrily said, "I am going to accept this coconut myself in order to honour Raṇamalla, the king of Jodhpur. But remember that the son born to this girl will be the heir to the throne."

The prince, Caṇḍa was not a bit sad, after hearing his father's word. He like Bhīṣma, roaringly said, "Respected father! I, touching your feet, take an oath that the son born to my new mother, will be the heir to the throne and throughout my life I'll remain engaged to do good to him." Having heard his promise, all the people praised him.

The twelve year old princess was married to the fifty year old Rāṇā Lākhā. She gave birth to a son who was named 'Mukula'. When Mukula was only five years old, the Muslims attacked Gaya, the place of pilgrimage. The Rāṇā prepared his army. It was vain to expect to return alive from the battle-field. Moreover a long distance had to be covered on foot. So the Rāṇā said to the prince, Caṇḍa, "Dear son! I am going to protect righteousness. What arrangement will be made for the livelihood of your younger brother 'Mukula'?"

Caṇḍa said, "He is the heir to the throne of Chittaur." Rāṇā did not want to enthrone a five year old boy. He wanted to convince Caṇḍa but Caṇḍa was firm in his vow. He enthroned Mukula in Rāṇā's presence and first of all honoured him himself.

Rāṇā Lākhā went for war and didn't return. Caṇḍa, having enthroned Mukula, administered the affairs of the state. His administration promoted joy and prosperity in the public. In spite of this, Mukula's mother doubted that Caṇḍa himself wanted to be enthroned by dethroning Mukula. Having heard this, Caṇḍa was very sad. He went to her and said, "Dear mother! I am leaving Chittaur in order to satisfy and please you; but whenever you need my service, send the message and I'll immediately come back."

When Caṇḍa had gone away, Mukula's mother called her brother from Jodhpur to look after the state affairs. Afterwards Raṇamalla, the king of Jodhpur himself, with many courtiers and servants, came to Chittaur. After some days he was motivated by a mean idea. He began to conspire to usurp the kingdom of Chittaur by murdering his daughter's son. When the king Mukula's mother came to know about her father's conspiracy, she was very much grieved but she had no helper anywhere. She, having written a letter to Caṇḍa, craved forgiveness and called him to protect Chittaur. As soon as Caṇḍa received the message, he came back and made best of his

efforts. At last he was able to liberate Chittaur from the clutches of Raṇamalla, the king of Jodhpur. Raṇamalla and his helpers were killed while his son Bodhājī fled. Prince Caṇḍa rendered service to Rāṇā Mukula throughout his life.

Brave Boy, Pratāpa, Who Kept Promise

Mahārāṇā Pratāpa was born in 1540. He was Mahārāṇā Udaya Singh's eldest son. He was educatec nd initiated according to the royal tradition of Mewar. He gained skill and mastery in the science of arms and weapons, in commanding army, in hunting and in administrating the affairs of the state in his boyhood. Udaya Singh loved his younger son, Jagamala very much and so he decided to declare him as the heir to the throne. Pratāpa was obedient and devoted to his father, therefore he did not oppose his father's decision in the least. Lord Rāma was the model for him, Who, having obeyed His father, renounced the kingdom and accepted to be exiled. From his boyhood he was pinched to see that his motherland was tormented in the fetters of slavery of the foreigners. He always reflected upon, how to free his motherland from their clutches. His maternal uncle, Rao Akṣayarāja always supported him and encouraged him. He was doubtful, lest Pratāpa should become a pray to the conspiracies of the harem and thus

his pious determination of freeing his motherland might be left in the lurch. Pratāpa was a very courageous boy. He was every inch a hero and a freedom fighter. Sometimes Pratāpa in his boyhood, alighting from the horse, with great faith and reverence, having a round of the victory-pillar of Mahārāṇā Kumbha, and smearing his forehead with the holy dust of Mewar, used to say, "If I have been suckled by my mother, belonging to a Kṣatriya caste (warrior class), and if in my blood there is a flow of the vigour of Mahārāṇā Sā̃gā, O victory-pillar! I, having taken an oath of freedom and patriotism, tell you and assure you that you will ever remain elevated being the symbol of victory of the glory of Sisaudia family. The enemy can't desecrate you with his touch while I am alive."

Rāṇā Sā̃gā was ever a model for Pratāpa in his boyhood. While paying homage he used to say, "I'll complete the mission left incomplete by Mahārāṇā Sā̃gā. I aim at translating into practice his dream of victory over Delhi. The day is not afar when the emperor of Delhi will beg alms from the descendants of Sā̃gā."

Pratāpa in his childhood proved that the head of the offspring of Bāppā Rāwala can't bow before any man. The boy, Pratāpa had taken an oath, not to get kingdom, but to liberate the country.

Brave Boy, Bādala

At that time Alauddin Khilaji ruled over Delhi as a king. He was a very cunning and cruel king. In Rājapūtānā, Rāṇā Ratana Singh ruled over Chittaur. Alauddin came to know that the Rāṇā's queen was very beautiful. He wanted to get the queen, Padminī somehow or the other. So he went to Rājapūtānā with a big army and camped at a little distance from Chittaur. That cunning fellow sent a message to the Rāṇā, "I'll come back after seeing Padminī's reflection in the mirror." Rāṇā Ratana Singh did not think it proper to shed blood for such a trivial matter. So he invited Alauddin to the fort and showed him the reflection (image) of Padminī in the mirror. Rāṇā came outside the fort to bade him good-bye. Outside the fort, Alauddin had concealed his soldiers. They attacked Rāṇā, caught him and took him to their camp as a captive.

When Rāṇā was made a captive, there was a cry of distress in the fort of Chittaur. The army of Alauddin was so big that by waging a battle, there was no hope to get victory over his army. At last queen Padminī's maternal uncle, Gorā made a plan. Alauddin was sent a message that the queen, Padminī, was ready to come to him, if he released Rāṇā. Seven hundred maid servants would also accompany her. So the royal soldiers should not check them. King Alauddin enthusiastically accepted the proposal. In the evening when it grew dark, seven hundred palanquins passed by. The soldiers of the king were celebrating the function intoxicated with victory.

Do you think that queen Padminī went to the Muslim king, by sitting in one of the palanquins? No, it was twelve year old Bādala, the nephew to Padminī, who had disguised himself as queen Padminī, armed with weapons. In other palanquins also there were Rājapūta warriors and the coolies, who were carrying the palanquins, were also warriors. They liberated Rāṇā and sent him towards the fort with some soldiers and they attacked Alauddin's army. Gorā was the commander of the army. Bādala showed wondrous heroism in this battle. But how long could a handful of Rājapūta warriors fight against the huge army of Alauddin?

Gorā died a heroic death. The boy, Bādala, slaughtering the Muslim soldiers fearlessly, entered the fort. Alauddin did not want the news to be conveyed in the fort. He wanted to capture Padminī and carry her to Delhi. But the twelve year old boy failed his strategy. As soon as the news reached the fort, the Rājapūta warriors came out enthusiastically

to sacrifice their lives for righteousness and for their motherland. Alauddin had to face a lot of difficulty in getting victory over them. When, having sacrificed most of his warriors in the battle, he entered the fort, he saw that a very big pyre was burning like wild fire. The brave women of Rājapūtānā, having entered the burning fire, had attained paradise in order to escape the touch of a sinful person. So Alauddin's sinful effort was all in vain. This glorious divine land of Bharat will ever remain illumined with the radiance of chaste women who burnt themselves in order to maintain their chastity and also by Bādala's heroism and sacrifice.

Brave Boy, Pratāpa

This boy is not Mahārāṇā Pratāpa, but he was an ordinary Rājapūta boy of Chittaur. He liked music very much. His parents and friends were not pleased with him. All people scolded and teased him by saying, "You are a Rājapūta and you don't know how to use a sword. How will you discharge your duty when the country is in crisis. What is the utility of a Rājapūta (a member of the warrior class), if he does not serve his country and stake his life for the country?

Pratāpa said to those people, "The country is not served only with a sword but also by music. I'll prove at the time of crisis that I am in no way less heroic than anybody else."

No one believed him. People thought that he was not only delicate but also boastful. But Pratāpa did not pay heed to what they said.

Delhi was ruled by the Moghul king. The Moghuls with a big army attacked Chittaur. But the fort of Chittaur was so strong that the Moghul army could not get victory over it. The Moghuls wanted to break the gates or walls of the fort,

but they had to go back because the Rājapūta warriors were shooting arrows and were injuring them.

The brave Rājapūtas had joined Mahārāṇās army. But Pratāpa was a boy and he did not know how to use weapons and missiles. So he did not join the army, but he sang the heroic songs in the army and encouraged warriors to fight bravely and sacrifice their life for the country. Moreover he encouraged the youths of the country to join the army by his heroic songs. The effect of his songs was that Mahārāṇā's army was doubled in number.

One day when Pratāpa was singing heroic songs, playing on his guitar, a Moghul soldier, being concealed, heard his song. That soldier caught Pratāpa and took him to his commander. The Moghul commander was very much pleased with him and said to him, "O boy! you will have to sing a song for us."

Pratāpa said, "It is my hobby to sing songs. I am ready to sing." The Moghul commander with his well armed army came near the fort of Chittaur. He asked Pratāpa to stand near the gate of the fort and sing a song.

The Moghul commander thought that, having heard Pratāpa's song, the soldiers inside the fort would think that another Rājapūta army had arrived to help them and therefore they would open the gate of the fort. Pratāpa understood the trick of the Moghul commander. He sang such a song that the warrior inside the fort became alert. They began showering arrows and stones on the Moghul army. Many Moghul soldiers were killed. The Moghul commander, scoldingly said to Pratāpa, "O boy! What are you singing?"

Pratāpa fearlessly said, "I am telling the warriors that the enemy is standing at the gate. So don't be cheated, be alert, don't open the gate but shower stones and crush the enemy mercilessly."

The Moghul commander at once cut Pratāpa's head but the Rājapūta warriors had become alert and so the Moghul army had to return disappointed. The next day the Rājapūtas found Pratāpa's dead body. The Mahārāṇā himself put the body of that boy, who had sacrificed his life for the sake of his country, on the pyre.

Brave Boy, Rāma Singh

Brave Raṭhore Amar Singh is famous for his radiance. He held a high rank in king Shahajahan's court. One day the king's brother-in-law named Salawat Khan insulted him. Amar Singh cut off his head in the court itself. No one had courage to check him or to utter any word against him. The Muslim courtiers fled here and there. Amar Singh came back home.

Amar Singh's brother-in-law's name was Arjuna Gaur. He was a man of very greedy and mean nature. Being induced by the king, he, having cheated Amar Singh, took him to the king's palace. When Amar Singh was passing through a small gate, Arjuna Gaur attacked him and killed him. The king Shahajahan was very much pleased at this news. He ordered to put the dead body of Amar Singh on a turret. Thus the corpse of a famous hero was left on the turret so that kites and crows could eat it.

When Amar Singh's wife heard the news, she decided to burn herself on the funeral pyre of her husband. But how could this act be possible without the corpse of her husband? She requested the few

Rājapūtas, that were there, to bring the corpse of her husband. But no one had the courage to bring the dead body because it was an offence to the king. At last she took a sword and was ready to bring her husband's corpse herself.

At that very moment Amar Singh's nephew named Rāma Singh, with a naked sword, come there and said, "Aunt! you need not go. I am going. Either I'll bring the corpse of my uncle or I'll be killed."

Rāma Singh was the son of Amar Singh's elder brother, Jasavant Singh. He was a youth of 15. His aunt blessed him. He rode the horse and directly reached the king's palace. The gate of the palace was open. The gate keeper could not recognize him and he entered the palace. But when he reached under the turret, hundreds of Muslim soldiers surrounded him. Rāma Singh was not worried about his death. He was catching the rein of the horse with his mouth and attacking the enemy with swords which he was holding in both of his hands. His whole body was stained with blood. There were thousands of Muslim soldiers. Rāma Singh was killing them and was proceeding ahead. He, crossing the dead bodies of the Muslim soldiers, climbed the turret. He put his uncle's corpse on his shoulder, and attacking the enemy

with the sword holding in one hand, climbed down. He rode the horse, with the corpse and went out of the gate of the fort before the other Muslim soldiers arrived there.

His aunt was standing, waiting for her nephew. Having received her husband's corpse, she prepared the funeral pyre and she herself sat on it. She blessed Rāma Singh—"Dear son, he who endangers his life in order to protect cows, Brāhmaṇas (members of the priest class), righteousness and chaste women, God gets pleased with him. You have maintained my prestige. Your fame will ever remain immortal in the world."

Brave, Fearless Boy, Śivājī

Śivājī, who became the protector of righteousness, had to face many difficulties in his boyhood. He was born in 1630 in the fort of Shivanera. His father, Śāhajī was in service in Bijapur court. When his father, Śāhajī was involved in the battle of Ahmed Nagar on behalf of the baron (Muslim Feudal Lord) of Bijapur, Māladār Khān, in order to please the emperor of Delhi, wanted to make the boy Śivājī and his mother Jījābāī captive and put them in the fort of Singh garha but his wicked plan did not bear fruit. Early three years of childhood of Śivājī spent in his own fort of Shivaner. After that, because of the fear of the enemies. Jījābāī with her son had to flee from one fort to the other constantly. But in spite of such adverse circumstances, the brave mother went on imparting military training to her son.

Jījābāī narrated the heroic tales of Rāmāyaṇa, Mahābhārata and Purāṇa (scriptures) to Śivājī. His teachers were Nāro, Trīmala, Hanumanta and Gomājī and his patron was very valiant Dādājī Koḍadeva. The result of education (training) was that Śivājī at a very small age became fearless and irrepressible. He made a group of small brave boys and, leading this group, played games of war. In his childhood he took a vow to protect righteousness, temples and cows.

Śāhajī had a desire that his son should become subservient to the king of the Bijapur state. When Śivājī was only 8 years old, one day his father took him to the royal court. Śivājī's father thought that, having seen the magnificence and splendour of the court, he would be attracted to it. But Śivājī did not pay any heed to the magnificence at all. When they reached the king, his father, patting his back, said, "Son, salute the king."

The boy turned his face toward his father and said, "He is not my king. I'll not bow down to him."

This utterance caused sensational atmosphere in the court. The king gazed at him but Śivājī did not bow his head, Śāhajī with scared looks, prayed, "Oh emperor! Forgive him, he is ignorant." He ordered his son to go back home. The boy turned and fearlessly went out of the court. When Śāhajī came back home, he scolded his son for his insolence. Then the son replied, "Father, why did you take me to the court? You know that I can't bow my head to any one else besides goddess Tulajā and you." Śāhajī became quiet.

After four years another incident happened. At that time Śivājī was twelve years old. One day Śivājī was walking along the main road of Bijapur. He saw that a butcher was carrying a cow and beating it with a stick because it did not want to go ahead, it was belching and was looking around with despair and solicitation. The Hindus saw this scene with bowed eyes but no one had courage to oppose the cruel act because their ruler was a Muslim. People were surprised to see when Śivājī took out his sword from the case, cut the string of the cow and freed it. Before the butcher uttered any word, Śivājī cut his head off.

When the news was conveyed to the king, he was furious with anger and he said to Śāhajī, "Your son seems to be very rowdy. Send him away somewhere out of Bijapur."

Śāhajī carried out the king's order. Śivājī was sent to his mother. But at last it was an auspicious day, when the king of Bijapur invited Śivājī, who had become the emperor of the free Hindu empire, to his kingdom, and when Śivājī reached the court of Bijapur, riding his elephant, passing along the route, the king of Bijapur gave him a warm welcome and bowed to him.

Brave Boy, Chatrasāla

Campata Rao, the king of Pannā was a man of righteousness and self-respect. His son, Chatrasāla was born in Vikrama Saṁvat 1706 in the forest of More hill. The Moghul king, Śāhajahān's army was making an effort to surround the area. So it was inevitable for them to conceal themselves. Therefore at Chatrasāla's birth, no function was celebrated. The enemies came so near, that people had to flee here and there to save their life. When this stampede ensued, the baby Chatrasāla was left all alone in the field. But by God's grace, he was saved because the enemy did not see him. Upto the age of four he had to live in the house of his maternal grandfather and then upto the age of seven he could live with his father. When he was five, he saw the idols of Lord Rāma and Lakṣmaṇa in the temple. He wanted to play with them and it is said that really Lord Rāma and Lakṣmaṇa played with him. After the death of his father; upto the age of thirteen Chatrasāla had to stay in his maternal grand father's house. After that he came back to Pannā; and his uncle, Sujāna Rāo imparted him military training very carefully. He acquired heroism as a paternal gift. He fulfilled the resolve of his father and Pannā state was blessed by having such a hero as Chatrasāla.

Aurangajeb was ruling over the throne of Delhi. His injustice was terrorizing the entire country. Chatrasāla at that time was about 13 or 14 years old. A fair in honour of the goddess of Vindhyavāsinī was held. There was hustle and bustle all around. People from afar were coming to have a vision of the goddess. King Sujāna Rāo was busy in talking with Bundele lords. Prince Chatrasāla put off his shoes, washed his hands and feet and went to the garden to pluck flowers to worship the goddess. Some other Rājapūta boys of his age also accompanied him. In the meanwhile some Muslim soldiers came there, riding horses. They alighted from their horses and asked, "Where is the temple of Vindhyavāsinī?"

Chatrasāla asked them, "Do you want to worship the goddess?"

The Muslim baron said, "Pooh! We have come to break down (destroy) the temple."

Chatrasāla handed over the basket of flowers to his companion and roaringly cried, "Talk sensibly. If you make such an utterance again, I'll pull out your tongue." The baron laughed and said, "What can you or your goddess do?" He had not completed the sentence yet, that Chatrasāla's sword thrust him through. There was a fight in the garden. The boys, who had no swords, ran away to bring swords.

This news reached the temple. The Rājapūtas put on their armour and took their swords but they saw that prince Chatrasāla was wielding a blood stained sword in one hand and in the second hand he was holding a basket of flowers and he was coming, smiling. His clothes were stained with blood. The prince all alone killed the enemy-soldiers. The king, Sujāna Rao embraced Chatrasāla, Goddess Vindhyavāsinī was pleased, having received the heroic flowers of his true priest.

Brave Boy, Durgādāsa Rathore

The protector of she-camels sent the message to the king of Jodhpur, Yaśavanta Singh that an ordinary farmer's son had killed a she-camel. The king ordered his soldiers to catch and bring that farmer to him. The name of the farmer was Āsakarana. He was a Rathore Rājapūta. The farmer said to the king, "Your Majesty, this is my son who has committed the crime."

The king angrily asked him, "Did you kill the she-camel?"

The boy fearlessly, accepting the crime, said, "Sir, I was protecting my field. When I saw the she-camels coming towards my field. I requested the grazier not to let them come towards my field. But he did not pay heed to what I said. If our crop is destroyed, what shall we eat? Therefore when one of the she-camels began to eat the corn in my field, I

killed it. Then other she-camels and the grazier fled."

It was difficult for the king to believe that a small boy could kill a strong she-camel. He asked the boy, "How did you kill the she-camel?"

The boy saw here and there. A camel was passing by at a little distance. He went to the camel, drew his sword and cut the neck of the camel. The camel fell down. The king was very much pleased with that boy. He (employed) him under him. This boy became a historical character, named Durgādāsa, famous for his bravery. He protected Yaśavanta Singh's queen and the prince Ajīta Singh from the cruel clutches of Aurangajeb. He liberated the state of Marawar from the clutches of the Muslims.

Brave Boy, Putta

Once Akbar, the king of Delhi came to Chittaur to get victory over it. The Rāṇā of Chittaur, being terrified, fled and his commander named Jayamala began to protect the city. But a night Akbar Shah shot him dead, firing a gun. The people of Chittaur were then very much frightened. But in the meanwhile a brave boy declared that he would protect his country.

The name of that brave boy was Putta. He was only 16 years old. Though he was a boy, yet he was very courageous and brave. His mother, sister and wife happily allowed him to go to the battle-field. Not only this, but they also, wielding weapons, very enthusiastically, reached the battle-field to protect their country.

Akbar's army was divided into two battalions. One battalion was fighting against Putta while the second battalion was coming to check him. This second battalion was wonderstruck, having perceived the bravery of Putta's mother, wife and sister. At about 2 p.m. when Putta reached to them, he saw that his sister had died a heroic death and his mother and wife were badly wounded. Having seen Putta, his mother said,

"Dear son, we are going to heaven. Protect your motherland, fighting bravely or dying a

heroic death, meet us in heaven." Having uttered these words, she breathed her last. His wife, looking at him patiently, with unblinking eyes, died bravely. Now Putta with extraordinary zeal and heroism fought against the enemy. He carried out the order of his mother and fought very enthusiastically against the enemy. Finally he sacrificed his life for his motherland by fighting zealously. Thus four valiant members of a family went to heaven and their glory will never fade in the world.

Brave Boys, Ajīta Singh and Jujhāra Singh

Guru Govinda Singh was staying in the fort of Anandapur. There were some sikh soldiers with him. But the Muslim army, in which there were twenty times more soldiers than the Sikh army, surrounded the fort. The food material was going to be exhausted. The leaders of the army requested Gurujī earnestly, "Kindly, go away quietly from here with your children. You should save your life in order to save the country from the tyranny of the cruel enemies."

When his companions insisted very much, one mid-night he, with his mother, wife and four sons, left the fort quietly. But he had not gone afar to a safe place, that the Muslim army came to know this fact. The soldiers on foot and riding on horses, ran in search of them, in all directions with lamps. The result of their hectic search was that Guru Govinda Singh, his wife and two sons, Ajīta Singh and Jujhāra Singh were separated from other members, Gurujī's mother and two younger sons, Jorāwara Singh and Fataha Singh.

The Sikh soldiers came out of the fort and

attacked the Muslim army so that Gurujī could reach a safe place. In the dark night a terrible battle was fought. The Sikh soldiers, whose number was small, were fighting staking their lives. But the Muslim soldiers were chasing Gurujī. The soldiers, who accompanied Gurujī, had been killed by fighting bravely. The eldest son named Ajīta Singh of Gurujī could not bear this sight. He went to his father and bowing down to him, he said, "Dear father, our soldiers are staking their lives to protect us. Under such circumstances I don't want to flee. Kindly allow me to fight."

Having heard the suggestion of his son, Gurujī embraced him and said, "Dear son! you are blessed. Those, who sacrifice their lives to save their country and righteousness, become immortal. Discharge your duty by fighting."

Ajīta Singh, with a few soldiers, made a fierce and sudden attack on the enemy. But how could the few soldiers fight against the big army? They killed hundreds of soldiers of the enemy-army and then died heroic deaths. When the eldest brother fell down in the battle, his younger brother, Jujhāra Singh, bowing down to his father, said, "Kindly allow me to follow the footsteps of my elder brother."

Blessed are the sons who are eager to sacrifice their lives for their country and for righteousness;

and blessed is the father who blesses and allows his sons happily to make such a sacrifice. Gurujī blessed Jujhāra Singh and said, "Go and fight, son, the gods are waiting for you; attain immortality."

Jujhāra Singh also pounced upon the enemy with the few remaining soldiers. The fatigued and starved Sikh-soldiers, under the leadership of the boy, Jujhāra Singh killed so many soldiers of the enemy-army that the remaining soldiers lost courage to chase Gurujī. But finally, fighting bravely against the enemy, Jujhāra Singh and his soldiers died heroic deaths.

Brave Boy, Pṛthvī Singh

A hunter caught a terrible lion from the forest and kept it in an iron cage. He brought it to the Moghul King, Aurangajeb of Delhi. The lion was roaring again and again. The king said, "There can't be available a bigger and more terrible lion than this."

The courtiers of the king supported his statement but Yaśavanta Singhjī said, "Sir, I have a lion who is more powerful than this lion." The king was very much enraged. He said, "Bring your lion and let both the lions fight. If your lion is defeated, your head will be cut off." Yaśavanta Singh agreed.

The next day a big iron box of strong bars was put infront of the fort of Delhi for the purpose of the fight between two lions. A big crowd assembled there to see the fight. King Aurangajeb also arrived at the right time and sat on the throne. Yaśavanta Singh accompanied by his ten year old son, Pṛthvī Singh came there.

Seeing him, the king asked, "Where is your lion?"

Yaśavanta Singh said, "Sir, I have brought my lion with me. Kindly, permit to begin the fight."

With the order of the king that wild lion was left in the big cage which was meant for the fight. Yaśavanta Singh ordered his ten year old son to enter the cage. The king and the people assembled there, were wonderstruck but the ten year old boy, Pṛthvī Singh, having bowed down to his father, smiling, entered the cage.

The lion gazed at Pṛthvī Singh. Having seen the radiant eyes of the boy, the lion withdrew itself but the hunters with the tip of a spear instigated the lion. That lion being enraged, roaringly, pounced upon Pṛthvī Singh. Pṛthvī Singh moved aside and drew his sword.

When Yaśavanta Singh saw his son, drawing his sword, he addressing him, said, "What are you going to do. The lion has no sword, will you attack the lion with a sword? It is unjust."

Having heard his father's utterance, Pṛthvī Singh threw his sword and pounced upon the lion. This brave boy caught the jaws of the lion and tore them and then tore the whole body

of the lion into two pieces.

All the people, assembled there, showered congratulations and acclamations on the brave boy, Pṛthvī Singh. When Pṛthvī Singh, stained with blood, came out of the cage, Yaśavanta Singh lovingly embraced him.

Brave Boy, Jālima Singh

Nawab Sarafaraj ruled over Murshidabad. He could not win over the love of his subjects. Therefore a conspiracy was made against him.

The name of the conspirator was Aliworthy Khan. He with a big army went to fight against him. Seeing the big army, Sarafaraj was terrified but there was no way out except the fight (battle).

Both the armies had camped in the famous Giriya plain. In between, the holy Ganges was flowing, making a rippling sound. The reflection of the tents in the water of the Ganges looked splendid.

The night passed. In the morning the conchs and trumpets for the battle blared forth and the battle started.

Sarafaraj Khan was sitting on the elephant. His chief commander had been killed. So he was proceeding farther bravely. But suddenly a bullet struck him and he fell down. In his army it was only he who lost his life.

There was a Rājapūta warrior named Vijaya Singh in Sarafaraj army. He was incharge for the protection of the rear. He was stationed at Khamara near Giriya. He heard the news of the death of his master, his blood boiled and he, with full force, threw a lance aiming at Aliworthy but in the meanwhile a soldier of the hostile army shot him dead with a gun.

Vijaya Singh had a son, who was only 9 years old. His name was Jālima Singh. When Vijaya Singh, rolling down, fell on the ground from his horse, his son with a naked sword in his hand went to protect the dead body of his father. All around there was acclamation of the victory of Aliworthy. There was tumultuous sound of the battle drums all around but that nine year old boy did not get a bit scared.

He, with a small sword in his hand, roared like a cub. He was moving *to and fro,* fearless without caring for his life, so that any Muslim could not touch the body of his father. The enemies surrounded him from all sides but he did not swerve at all. He moved his small sword all around. Aliworthy Khan himself was present there. He was wonderstruck, having seen the

wonderful courage and also devotion of the boy to his father. He ordered his soldiers to perform the proper cremation of Vijaya Singh's dead body.

The soldiers, being pleased with the boy's bravery, carried him on their shoulders. The boy performed the cremation ceremony of his father on the bank of the holy Ganges and caused the ashes to flow in the holy Ganges.

The ashes flowed with the rippling sound of the Ganges and the boy came back with a sad heart to the text.

In the history of Murshidabad, Giriya battle is very famous. The wonderful bravery of a Rājapūta boy has made it more famous.

The place where Jālima Singh showed his bravery, is known as 'Jālima Singh's place of bravery."

Brave Boy, King of Jerāpur State

Near Hyderabad there was a small Hindu state, named Jerāpur. In the rebellion (freedom struggle) of 1857, the king of Jerāpur made an army of Rohila-Pathans in order to fight against the Britishers but at that time the king was only a boy. The minister of Hyderabad Nijam, named Salarajang, fraudulently arrested him and handed over to the Britishers.

The king loved a British Officer, named Colonel Metoja Taylor. The king called him 'Appā'. Colonel Taylor went to see the king in the jail and tried to seduce him, "If you mention the names of the persons who are involved in the rebellion, you will be pardoned."

But true and brave boys don't betray their companions. The king, smiling, said, "Appā! I'll not mention any name. I'll not endanger their lives in order to save my life. I don't want to ask for pardon. I don't like to live alive like a coward at the mercy of others."

Colonel Taylor said, "Do you know that you will be sentenced to capital punishment?" The boy-king said, "Yes, I know this fact, but if you accept my request, don't hang me to death. I am not a thief. Shoot me with a cannon and see that I will remain standing before the cannon patiently and quietly, without being terrified at all."

On the recommendation of Colonel Taylor, regarding the king as a boy, he was sentenced to transporation for life. Having heard this sentence, the king said, "Such punishment as imprisonment and transportation will not be liked even by a pauper hilly man while I am a king. I prefer death to transportation." The king snatched a pistol with a jerk from a British guard and shot himself with it. Having seen the bravery of a tender boy, the Britishers had to praise him for his heroic deed.

Boy, Socrates in Search of Truth

The boy, Socrates was born in the city Athens, in Greece in 469 B.C. His mother's name was Phinerita. His father, Afroniskasa was a common man who played on some instrument in accompaniment. After working hard throughout the day, he brought up his small family. Their economic condition was not good. The boy, Socrates for some days received free education in school and gymnasium. He was very much interested in music and science. Athens was the abode of great scholars, artists, philosophers, poets and musicians. The boy, Socrates liked to keep company with them. So he used to roam in their vicinity from morning till evening. The people were suddenly influenced by his ugly appearance (body), flat nose, big nostrils, clumsy face and large eyes. Though being poor, being dressed in rags, bare footed, he wandered in the whole city, yet his sharp talent, philosophical seriousness and eagerness

could not be concealed in his childlike agility. Gradually people were attracted towards him. The boy, Socrates possessed a very simple and loving nature. Because of poverty, when he was hungry, he did not hesitate at all in taking meal at his friends' houses.

The boy, Socrates was so much lost in reflecting upon the truth that he was oblivious of taking meal. His eagerness for knowledge was gradually enhanced. He did not like to go outside Athens under any circumstances. He never went to forests and gardens. This mentality of his boyhood was an introduction to his desireless and serious future philosophical life. Great men's boyhood is uncommon in this way. Along the road or at the crossing, wherever he saw a crowd of people, he reached there and started discussing knowledge (wisdom).

The name of his preceptor was Pradix. He loved Socrates. The elderly people of Athens loved Socrates as their own child.

The boy, Socrates had an aversion to prosperity and pleasures and so he ever remained afar from them. He regarded falsehood as a deadly sin. According to him it was a serious crime to think ill of others.

In his boyhood he felt as if he had been sent to this mortal world to accomplish some divine task. Undoubtedly that divine task was the careful study of truth. By nature he was religious-minded. He never did any work against his conscience.

Once from morning till evening, standing on the road, he went on reflecting upon some topic and it continued even throughout the night. When some people saw him, they lay down spreading their mats to see, when he would stop reflecting upon some topic. Intellectual Socrates went on thinking till next morning and in the morning bowing down to the sun, he went back home. This incident indicates his life of great perseverance and self-control. In fact he was a great thinker. In the later stage of his life, he admitted that during his boyhood he liked to reflect upon the questions—'What is Prakṛti (Nature)? What is God? How does the universe originate and dissolve?' The city, Athens was his school and moving beings were his teachers. How fascinating and encouraging his boyhood was! The great aim of his life was "to Know thy own self."

Truthful Napoleon Who Shared Others' Sufferings

In the capital of Corsica, in a garden, a boy and a girl were playing. The boy was Napoleon and the girl was Ilaija. While playing, they went away far from the garden. There because of Ilaija's negligence, a farmer's daughter's basket full of ripe fruit, fell down and the pieces of fruit were broken. Seeing her weeping, Ilaija said, "Brother! Let us run away so that no one may know."

Napoleon said, "I'll not go. Just see the condition of the girl that she is weeping. We should make up for her loss. It is our duty." Having said so, Nepoleon went to that girl. Seeing her brother, Ilaija also went there and began to pick up the fallen pieces of fruit.

"What explanation shall I give to my mother? The whole lot of the fruit has been spoiled. I would have earned my meals for three days with the contents of this basket." Having said so, that girl began to weep bitterly. "Don't weep," having said so, Napoleon gave her three small coins of silver and said to her, "Come to my house and

the remaining amount I'll pay you there." Ilaija slowly said to her brother, "O brother! What are you doing? When our mother comes to know this fact, she'll, as punishment, give us only bread and water."

The brother replied—'It does not matter. We

have spoiled her fruit, so we'll have to pay for them."

In the meanwhile, the maid servant called them, and they ran away to her. She saw that a girl was following them. She asked, "Who is she?"

The boy replied, "We have spoiled some pieces of her fruit. The mother will pay her—thinking so, I have brought her here."

In the drawing room, Napoleon's mother, Madam Liticia was sitting. Napoleon, Ilaija, the maid servant and the farmer's daughter reached there. Addressing her children, she said, "Had I not told you, not to go outside the garden? Now you will not be allowed to go to play."

"Mother, don't punish Ilaija, I went outside the garden and she only accompanied me." Having said so, Napoleon accepted his fault. Ilaija, being silent, began to look at her brother's face. Madam Liticia's brother was also sitting there. Being pleased with the boy's truth, he requested his sister to pardon him for his offence.

Frightened Ilaija was encouraged with the behaviour of her brother and she, holding the hand of her maternal uncle, said, "It was by my mistake that the loss has been sustained. My brother is not at fault."

Her maternal uncle asked, "What did you do, Ilaija?" She narrated the whole incident and accepted that it was her mistake and she was responsible for the loss. Her eyes filled with tears. As she accepted her offence her mother forgave her.

Then Napoleon requested his mother to give him three coins as his monthly pocket expenses. The mother gave him three coins and said that he would not be given his pocket expenses for one and a half months. Napoleon gave the coins to the fruit seller girl.

The farmer-girl was pleased, having received the full cost of her fruit and she began to return the three small silver coins to Napoleon which he had already paid to her. But Napoleon did not take it back. Madam Liticia was pleased with the good behaviour of that girl and she asked her, "Where is your mother? How many brothers and sisters are you? Where is your house?" and so on. Then all of them went to her house and they made arrangement of medicines and food for her sick mother.

Honesty of the Boy, Gokhale

The great patriot, Śrī Gopāla Kṛṣṇa Gokhale in his boyhood, when he studied in a school, one day the teacher gave him some questions to be solved at home. Gopāla Kṛṣṇa didn't know the answer of one of the questions, therefore he solved it with the help of some other student. The teacher checked the answer books of all the boys and found that only Gopāla Kṛṣṇa had answered (solved) all the questions correctly.

Having seen this, his teacher was very much pleased with him and he wanted to give him some prize. The boy, Gopāla Kṛṣṇa did not accept the prize but he began to weep. Seeing this, the teacher was very much surprised, and asked him, why he was weeping. The boy, with folded hands, very humbly, said, "Sir, you might have thought that I have solved all these questions myself. But it is not true. In one of these questions, I took help from a friend of mine. Now, Sir, you may judge whether I deserve prize or punishment."

Having heard this, the teacher was very much pleased with him, and awarding him the prize,

said, “I award you this prize for your honesty (truthfulness).”

Honesty of the Boy, Rānāḍe in the Game

In those days, on one of the full moonlit nights, there was a custom to invite Brāhmaṇas (members of the priest class) and friends to offer milk to them. That night all boys of the school were allowed to play 'Caupaḍa' (an Indian game played with three dice) upto 2 a.m. Once it so happened that no boy (son) of his father's friends came to play. The reason was that all of them had gone to a neighbouring village with some piece of work. His younger sister had also slept. He went to his father's sister to take 'Caupaḍa'. She said, "Durgā is sleeping and there is no other boy to play with you. With whom will you play?" Rānāḍe replied, "I'll play with someone or the other, please, give me 'Caupaḍa'." She gave him the 'Caupaḍa'. He took it and went into the porch and began to play. On one side he was the player and on the other side he began to play dice on behalf of the pillar. With one hand he played his dice and with the other hand he played the dice of the pillar. When he was defeated by the pillar twice, his father's sister, laughing at him, said, "O boy, you have been humiliated by defeat by even a lifeless pillar." At this the boy was not enraged and he said slowly, "It is O.K. Whatever is true, is true. The dice played with the hand of the pillar, made it victorious, while I was defeated. What is the matter

of humiliation in it? I played the dice of the pillar with the right hand which had the practice, while I played my dice with the left hand which had no practice to play the dice, so how could I be victorious?"

Had there been any other boy, he would have not accepted his defeat against a pillar. Thus Rānāḍe had formed the nature from boyhood that he was never deceptive but was ever true and frank.

Truth of the Girl, Victoria

From her childhood Victoria's parents tried their best to make her virtuous and modest. In the royal family, Victoria was the only offspring. Therefore it was predetermined that she would become the queen of England. Her mother, Luisa tried very carefully that her daughter should not be endowed with any evil. Victoria got her weekly pocket expenses which she usually spent in buying toys and distributing them to her companions. Her mother had advised her not to borrow nor to get into debt.

One day When Victoria was eight years old, she went to market with her female-teacher. They went to a toy-shop where Victoria liked a small box. Her money was with her teacher. The teacher told her that the money of that week had been spent. The shopkeeper said, "Please, take this box, money will be paid afterwards."

The girl, Victoria said, "I'll not borrow. My

mother has advised me not to borrow. Please, set this box apart. Next week when I receive pocket expenses, I'll take it, by paying you for it." After a week when she got money, she went to the shop and bought the box.

One day Victoria was not interested in studies.

Her teacher said, "Study a little and then I'll let you go."

The girl said, "I'll not study today."

The teacher said, "Obey me."

The girl insisted and said, "I'll not study."

Her mother Luisa heard it and raising the curtain came into that room and scolding her daughter, said, "Why do you prattle?"

The teacher said, "Madam, don't get angry, it is the first chance that she has not obeyed me."

The girl, Victoria, immediately holding the hand of her teacher, said—'you don't remember, this is the second time, I have disobeyed you."

It was her generous, determined and truthful nature of childhood that during her reign, she became such a renowned and favourite ruler of her subjects (public).

The Girl, Helena Walker's Fidelity to Truth

Two hundred years ago, the girl, Helena Walker was born in a poor family in Scotland. At that time a strict rule was in force, having broken which, the defaulter was sentenced to death.

Helena loved her younger sister very much and always kept her with her. Once this small girl broke the rule. Though this small girl was innocent and gentle, and she had not broken the rule intentionally, yet it was certain that she would be punished by the king for her offence.

It was an occasion of severe test for Helena. If she, as a witness, had given false testimony, her sister's life could have been saved without any doubt, and no one would have known that her sister had broken the rule.

But Helena had learnt the sacred lesson that in the world there is no other sin as deadly as 'to tell a lie.' She knew well, there was no penitence for that deadly sin. She had determined that she would not tell a lie, even if she had to risk her own life.

Her sister had a different nature. She tried to instigate Helena to save her life by telling a lie. She entreated Helena to show mercy but it was not an easy task to

deviate Helena from the truth. Her younger sister said to her, "You have a stony heart. I am going to be hanged to death and you are talking of justice and truth. If you lie a bit, my life will be saved." But she could not budge Helena.

Helena would not tell a lie but she was thinking to find out a way to save her younger sister from the clutches of death. An idea came to her mind that her sister's life could be saved, if the king granted a pardon to her. The most difficult task was that the king of Scotland lived in London which was hundreds of miles away from her place. Helena belonged to a poor family. In those days there were neither trains nor journeys were safe. The rich people went to London by horse-carriages. It was a problem how a poor girl would cover such a long journey. But she started her journey. She continued her journey throughout the night, through desolated forests, hazardous paths and in bitter cold, thinking of God, and finally she reached London. She got blisters on her soft feet due to excessive walking. She asked all over but it was all in order to protect truth and to be fully devoted to justice.

Helena went to the house of her father's friend who was a feudal chieftain. At that time the king was out of station. So Helena requested the feudal chieftain that she wanted to meet the queen, so he should help her. But he gave a flat denial. Helena did not lose heart but she had patience. She herself went to the queen and explained to her the reason of her coming to London. Truth is victorious. The queen was very much pleased with Helena's fidelity to truth and devotion to the state. She granted pardon to Helena's sister. Helena's truth pulled her sister out of the jaws of death.

Vīreśvara Mukhopādhyāya's Honesty

In Bengal, outside the city, Māldā, a boy of about 13 years was walking in a garden. In the meanwhile a traveller of Kabul named Bashir Mohammed, with his luggage, came there, stayed for sometime and then went away. But he had forgotten his money bag in which there was an amount of five thousand rupees. That Bengali boy picked up that bag and with honesty determined to return it to its real owner.

When Bashir Mohammed had covered some distance, he remembered that he had forgotten his money bag. He felt agitated and immediately went back to the garden. The boy, having seen him worried, asked him, "Have you lost anything?" The businessman said, "I have lost my money bag." The boy handed over his money bag to him. Bashir Mohammed counted the money and found that it was exactly the same. So he asked the boy, "How could you control yourself from being greedy for money?"

The boy humbly replied, "I have learnt the

lesson from my childhood that I should never steal the wealth of any one by regarding it as a clod of earth." Having listened to what the boy had said, the businessman was wonderstruck. He, being pleased with the honesty of the boy, wanted to give him five rupees as an award. But the boy said, 'It was my duty to return you your money. Why should I get an award? Had I not returned it to you, I would have been dishonest."

Having perceived that boy's honesty, Bashir Mohammed applauded his act and he got this news published in the newspapers. Having seen the boy's honesty, Bashir Mohammed said, "This money belonged to my Lord. Had the boy not returned the money, my Lord would have lost His faith in me and I would have been imprisoned. Therefore I cannot describe in words the good what this boy has done to me. I can never forget this boy and I'll pray daily to God—May God grant him a long and happy life!"

The name of that boy was Vīreśvara Mukhopādhyāya. Every man can become popular by his goodness (virtues) like this boy and can deserve blessings.

A True Boy Who Saved an Innocent Boy from Punishment

In a school while studying, some boys produced a whistling sound. One day the preceptor said, "If anybody whistles, he will be punished." So that day no one produced the whistling sound, but the next day again, the whistling sound was heard. In the school there was a notorious boy who used to whistle. The preceptor thought that he must have whistled. The preceptor asked him whether he had whistled. He said, "No". But the preceptor did not believe him. As soon as the preceptor, being angry with him, raised the cane to beat him, suddenly an another boy came, and admitting his offence, said, "Sir, he did not whistle, it was by mistake that the whistling sound was produced by me. Kindly, punish me."

The preceptor, being pleased with him, said, "You yourself have admitted your offence and saved another innocent boy from being punished. I am very much pleased with your honesty. All

the boys should speak the truth in the same way as you have spoken."

George Washington's Benevolence and Truth in Boyhood

Once on the bank of a hilly river, a woman was pitifully crying, "Save! Save my child!"

People came, running but no one had the courage to jump into the river because there was a strong current in the river and there were rocks in the river, if a person struck against those rocks, he would be smashed. In the meanwhile, an eighteen year old young man came running. He put off his coat hurriedly and jumped into the river with a thud.

People were beholding with unblinking eyes. Several times that young man was likely to be ensnared in the whirlpool. Many times he had a narrow escape from striking against rocks. It all happened in a few moments. Finally he was successful in bringing the drowning unconscious boy to the bank of the river, by loading him on his back. The boy, who staked his life to save the life of another boy, was—George Washington.

George Washington was the son of an American farmer. One day, when he was a small boy, his father gave him an axe. George began to play with it in the garden. He cut trees with it and laughed. His father had planted a fruit-tree which was very scarce. George cut it with the axe and went back home joyfully.

His father reached the garden and saw that the fruit-tree had been cut. He asked the gardeners whether they had cut that tree. They said, "No." Then having gone back home, he asked George. George said, "Daddy! I was playing and trying to test whether I could cut the tree with the axe and it was cut."

The father said, "Son! I didn't give you the axe for this purpose, but I am very much pleased with your truth. So I forgive you. I am very much pleased that you have spoken the truth."

George Washington became the well known President of America.

Truth of the Boy, Charley

A boy named Charley was going, tossing a ball in a city. At that time the ball struck the windowpane of the shop of a chemist and the windowpane was broken. Charley did not run

away from there because he was a brave and truthful boy. He went into the shop of the chemist and told him, "Your window pane has been broken by my mistake." The chemist said, "Get a new window pane fitted." The boy was poor, he said, "I have no money. But I'll earn some money by working as a labourer and then I'll get the new window pane fitted." Then he worked as a labourer at the chemist's shop for several days and earned the money for buying the window pane and paid it to the chemist. Having received the money, the chemist said, "You are an honest boy, I want to employ you as a work agent." That boy accepted the job and began to pass his life happily.

Honesty may be a bit hurtful at the beginning, but if it is maintained, finally it bears a sweet fruit.

The Boy Who Handed over Necklace to Its Owner

There was a sailor. In his family there were three members—he himself, his wife and his son. After the death of the sailor, his wife and son were left without support. The boy thought that he should earn his livelihood by doing some work. With the permission of his mother, he went in search of a job. Fortunately he got a job on a ship. Once his ship went to a big sea port. The boy always spoke the truth. He regularly prayed to God and was virtuous. So the captain of the ship was kind to him and other sailors liked him. One day that boy went to visit the city with other sailors. In the meanwhile, an officer and his wife alighted from a train. While that woman was alighting, her necklace fell down. No one else except that boy saw the necklace. That boy saw the necklace and picked it up at once. When his companions came to know this fact, they said to him, "Let us sell this precious necklace and get a lot of money, then there will remain no need of doing a job on the ship."

Having heard so, the boy said, "This necklace does not belong to us, it is of someone else. If we take it, we'll become thieves and it is a deadly sin to commit a theft. My mother says that a man can be cheated but God cannot be cheated because He is omnipresent. Therefore I'll return the necklace to its owner."

His companions tried their best to persuade him but he didn't agree with them. He returned the necklace to the lady who was its owner. That lady was very much delighted, having found out her necklace and she gave him a prize. When the captain of the ship heard this news, he began to love the boy more than usual. Who does not love truth?

The Boy Who Reformed Others with His Truth

A sailor's son had a job on a ship. All the sailors of that ship drank wine but only that boy did not drink wine. One day the captain of that ship was very much pleased with him and he offered the boy vintage wine but the boy refused the offer plainly and politely. The captain said, "Will you not carry out my order? If you don't obey me, I'll imprison you." The boy with folded hands said, "Sir, I don't want to disobey you but I want to express my inability as far as drinking wine is concerned." After this the captain scoldingly, said to him, "If you don't drink this cup of wine, you are going to be chained just now and you will be charged with disobedience." Having listened to these words of the captain, the boy, said weepingly, "Sir, I am disobeying you because I have given my word to my mother not to drink wine. My father died because he was addicted to drink. Therefore my mother has ordered me to take a pledge never to drink wine."

Having heard the boy's reply, the captain was wonderstruck and he said, "O, boy! You are

just. I am very much pleased with your resolve. I want people to follow in your footsteps. All people know that wine is a poison but they don't give up this habit of drinking wine. Therefore I also give up this habit of drinking wine from today." Having uttered these words, he threw the bottles of wine into the sea.

An Honest Poor Boy

In England in winter season it is very cold and there is snowfall. The poor people or poor boys have no houses to live because they can't pay high rent. In London such poor people earn their livelihood by selling petty articles such as match boxes etc.

One day a poor boy was standing near a hotel and selling match boxes. His clothes were torn, he was bare footed and he was trembling with cold. At that time two gentlemen passed that way. He said to them, "Sir, will you, kindly, buy a match box?" They said, "No." Then that boy said, "It costs only a penny, please." One of the two men said, "I don't need." The boy said, "Kindly, take two match boxes for a penny.

Then one of them said, "Give it to me." He put his hand into the pocket but there was no penny. So he said, "Sorry, I have no small change. Therefore I'll buy it tomorrow." The boy said, "Sir, take it today because I have nothing to eat today. I'll bring the small change. The gentleman gave him a shilling. He went to take the small change for a shilling but did not come back for sometime. The gentleman thought that the boy had gone away with the shilling and he went back home.

Next day the gentleman came to that street again and began to search that boy. In the meanwhile he came across that boy's younger brother. The boy asked the gentleman, "Did you buy the match box from my brother last evening?" The gentleman replied, "Yes, where is he?" The small boy said, "When he had gone to have small coins for a shilling, he met with an accident and was badly injured. He has lost his match boxes and your seven pennies in the accident. He could find out only four pennies. Kindly take these four pennies. He was admitted to the hospital. When I met him in the hospital, he narrated the incident to me and asked me to return these pennies to you." Then the gentleman asked the small boy, "Have you eaten anything?" The boy replied, "No". He provided some food to the boy and went to the hospital. In the hospital the boy was lying on the cot. Having seen the gentleman, the boy said, "Last evening when I was coming back with the small change for your shilling, I met with an accident and the coins fell down. Whatever I could find out, that I gave to my younger brother to return to you. I hope that he must have returned it to you."

Having said so, he said to his younger brother,

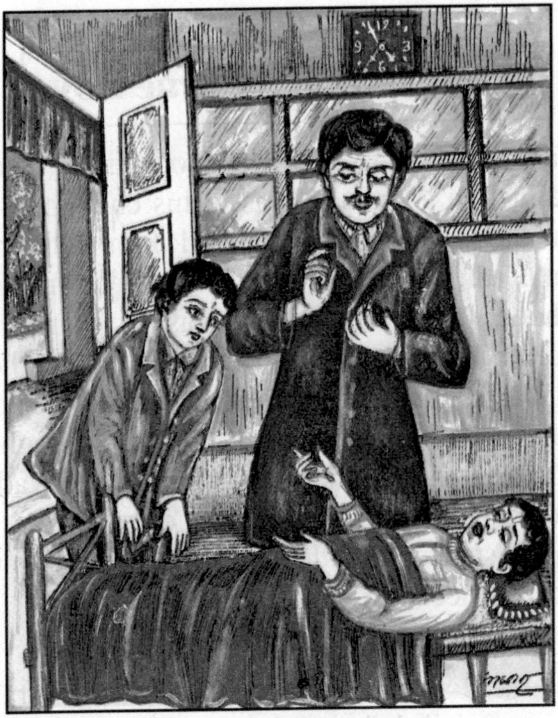

"Brother, now I am departing from this body. Who will look after you in my absence?" After the death of parents, I looked after you as much as I could, by doing labour. Now God will take care of you." Having heard so, that gentleman shouldered the responsibility of rearing his younger brother. The injured boy was very much pleased after hearing it and he left this world, begging God's mercy (grace).

Abdul Kadir, a True Boy

Saiyad Abdul Kadir was born in a village, Jīlāna in Iran. When he was in his childhood, his father died. His mother reared him. The boy, Abdul Kadir loved learning (education) from his childhood. In those days there was no arrangement to receive higher education in the neighbourhood of Jīlāna. Having received education in the local school, he decided to go to Baghdad, as Baghdad was the centre of higher education. Abdul Kadir's mother did not want to send her only son at such a long distance for education but she permitted him to go because he insisted on it.

It happened about nine hundred years ago when there were neither motors nor trains. Traders carried their goods on camels and ponies from one place to another in caravan because on the way there was fear of robbers and way layers. The travellers also went with the caravan of traders. A caravan of traders was going from Jīlāna to Baghdad. Abdul Kadir's mother stitched forty sovereigns in the waist coat, which was stuffed with cotton, carefully. When Abdul started with the caravan, his mother said, "My dear son! Your father left this money only, use it carefully. Follow my advice always that you should never tell a lie even in the period of crisis, and you should have faith in God's grace."

Bowing low to his mother, the boy, Abdul Kadir started with the traders. On the way robbers robbed the traders by attacking them, when they were passing through a deserted forest. They also beat them badly. The poor traders suffered all this helplessly as their number was small while the number of the waylayers was large. The waylayers saw that the boy, Abdul Kadir had nothing with him because he was dressed in tatters. When the waylayers, having robbed the traders, were departing, a waylayer by the way asked Abdul Kadir, "O boy! Have you any money?" Abdul Kadir remembered his mother's words and without hesitation said, "Yes, I have forty sovereigns."

The waylayers thought that the boy was making a joke. The waylayers scolded him but when Abdul Kadir, having put off his waist coat, showed forty sovereigns to them, they were wonderstruck. Their leader asked him, "O boy! Don't you know that we'll grab your sovereigns, then why have you disclosed this secret to us.?"

Abdul Kadir said, "My mother had advised me never to tell a lie. How could I tell a lie to save my sovereigns? If you grab my sovereigns, yet God will shower His grace on me and my work will be done."

Having heard the boy's utterances, the robbers repented of their misdeeds of robbery. They returned not only Abdul Kadir's sovereigns but also the money of the traders which they had robbed and gave up robbery for ever. Thus a boy, with the firm resolve of speaking the truth, saved the robbers from committing the crime of robbery.

Honesty of a Beggar-boy

A rich man was passing by a path. A poor boy, who was in a sorry plight, went to him and begged for money. The rich man took out a four anna coin from his pocket and, giving it to the poor boy, said, "Out of it, take an anna and return three annas to me." But the beggar-boy had no small change. He said, "I am going to bring the small change." Saying so, the boy left. The rich man waited for a short time and then went away. When the poor boy returned with the small change, he did not find the rich man there. He decided that he would return his three annas, when he again passed that way.

That boy earned his livelihood by begging but never used those three annas. After a week that rich man passed that way. That boy, having seen him, ran up to him and handed over three annas to him. That rich man did not remember the incident. He was very much pleased with the honesty of the poor boy. He took pity on him because of his pitiable condition. He took him home and admitted him to a school. The boy

studied and finally became a talented scholar. Thus he led a comfortable and reputed life.

Honesty of a Boy

Once a small boy went to his neighbour's house. In the neighbour's house, no one was there at that time. The boy saw that there were apples of good quality in a basket. But he did not think it proper even to touch those apples. The neighbour came back home and saw that there were all the apples in the basket as he had left them. He asked the boy, "Don't you like apples?"

The boy said, "I like apples very much."

The neighbour said, "Then why did you not steal apples when no one was here to see you?"

The boy said, "There might not be any one else besides me but I was there to see, and I did not want to see myself committing any crime such as theft etc., which is an act of dishonesty."

The neighbour was very much pleased with the reply of the boy. He gave several apples to the boy and said to him, "You are a very good boy. You should also know that God is omnipresent and He sees all our virtuous and sinful deeds. We should not perform any evil

deed, because we can't conceal it from God, Who is the master (lord) of the entire universe."

The Shepherd-boy Who Kept His Promise

In a village a shepherd-boy was grazing his goats, while sitting under a tree. Then he saw a twelve year old handsome and well dressed boy behind him. The shepherd boy thought that the boy should be the son of the watchman of the forest. So he saluted the well dressed boy and requested him to speak out what he wanted. The boy said "Are there any nests of birds in this forest?" The shepherd boy, somewhat being surprised, said, "Yes, sir, there are many nests in this forest. You are the son of the master of this forest, then why don't you know this?"

That handsome boy expressed desire to see the nest. The shepherd-boy said, "I have seen a fine nest today but I am unable to show it to you." In the meanwhile the teacher of that handsome boy reached there, and, having listened to what the shepherd-boy had said, spoke angrily, "You are very foolish. The prince has never seen a nest, therefore he wants only to see it, he'll not touch it, therefore please him by showing a nest."

The shepherd-boy said politely, "I am sorry that I can't show it to him." Having heard this, the teacher said, "O boy, you might have pleased many people, then why don't you please the prince?" Having heard this, the boy was wonderstruck. He, putting off his cap, bowing his head, said politely, "Is he a prince? I am very much pleased to see him and consider myself fortunate. But even if the king himself comes, I'll not be able to show the nest to him. The reason is that my friend, Mathurā grazes goats on that mountain. He showed me a fine nest this morning, but he had to do something with that nest. So he asked me not to show this nest to anyone else. I accepted his proposal and therefore I'll not break the promise." Having heard this, the teacher in order to put him to a test, took out a purse full of guineas from his pocket and said to the boy, "If you show the fine nest to the prince, you'll get all these guineas and Mathurā will know nothing."

Having heard this, the shepherd-boy said, "Whether Mathurā knows it or not, I'll not betray him. I'll never break my promise."

Having heard this, the teacher said, "Do you know the value of these guineas? You can buy a lot of things with these guineas."

The shepherd boy said, "Sir, I know that my parents will get rid of their poverty by receiving these guineas but I'll not do so. Kindly, don't induce me to be greedy."

Having heard this, the teacher said, "You may keep your promise. But I want to suggest that you should seek permission from your friend and then I'll give all these guineas to you; and if you want, you can also share them with your friend."

The shepherd-boy said, "O.K., I'll see after seeking permission." After it the teacher and the prince went home and having inquired about the shepherd boy, came to know that the shepherd-boy's name was Jīvo and his father was a very gentle person. Having come back with his friend, the shepherd-boy said, "My friend has permitted me to show the nest. Now I can show you the nest."

Then he called the prince near the nest and said, "Just see, the female bird is sitting on the eggs in the nest." As soon as he uttered these words, the female bird flew away and then they saw the well woven nest and the eggs joyfully. The prince was very much pleased. After it the teacher, as he had promised, gave some guineas to Mathurā and the remaining to Jīvo. Having taken those guineas, both the boys went home.

That day the king walking about, reached the same place in the forest to see his son. There they had tiffin and then the prince narrated the incident of the nest to the king and also the honesty of the shepherd-boy. Having heard the incident, the king was very much pleased with the boy and he called that shepherd-boy. When the shepherd-boy came, then the king lovingly asked him, "O boy! Do you want to study?" The boy said, "Sire, my father is a very poor man."

Then the king immediately called the shepherd and said to him, "The Government will bear all expenses for the education of your son. Therefore send him to the capital for studies."

The shepherd-boy went to the capital. He began

to study carefully and became well educated after sometime. The king employed him as a servant under him. Thus the boy became very happy and well known.

A Labour-boy's Honesty

One day a rich man called a labour-boy to clean down cobwebs. He began to clean down webs in a room which was well decorated. He was enjoying himself by seeing the decoration-pieces in the room. In the room he was all alone, so he began to see those pieces by picking them up. At that time he saw a very beautiful watch, set with jewels and diamonds. He picked up this watch and gazed at it. He was enticed by its beauty. He said to himself, "How fine it would have been, if he had got such a watch!" The sinful thought of stealing the watch came to his mind but, the next moment, he cried out. "Oh! What a sinful thought had come to my mind! If I am caught red handed while stealing, what a sad plight I'll have to face! The Government will punish me and imprison me. In the prison I shall have to break stones and indulge in such other drudgery. Once I lose honesty, no one will believe me and allow me to enter his house. Even if I am not caught red handed, I can't escape God's observation. My mother always says that we don't behold God but He always beholds us. We can't conceal any action from Him. He can see us even in the dark and even knows what comes to the mind."

Having said so, the boy's face fell, his body perspired and he began to tremble. Having put the watch at its original place, he uttered loudly, "Greed is a deadly sin. Greed induces a man to commit theft. Oh!

What had I to do with the watch of the rich people? Greed instigated me to commit this crime but gracious God saved me from doing so, because I remembered what my mother had advised me. Now, I'll never be greedy. In fact it is far better to remain poor, by following the righteous path, than to become rich by committing a theft. A thief can never sleep soundly and comfortably, howsoever rich he may be. Oh! It is the result of the thought of committing a theft that I am so much grieved. Had I committed the theft, it would have caused much more suffering to me." Having uttered so, he was again engaged in the work calmly.

The mistress was observing his activities and was listening to what he was saying. Suddenly she came to the boy and asked him, "O boy! Why have you not taken the watch?" Having heard her words, the boy was wonderstruck. He sat on the ground in a pitiable and helpless condition and began to tremble. He could utter no words, and his eyes filled with tears.

Having seen the pitiable condition of the boy, the mistress took pity on him and she said to him in a sweet voice, "Dear son, don't be terrified. I have listened to what you said. Inspite of being poor, you are so gentle, honest and you also fear God and righteousness. So I am very much pleased with you. Your mother is blessed that she has given you such a good advice. God is very much gracious to you that He saved you from getting entangled in the snare of greed. Son! Beware of greed. I am going to make arrangement for your board and books etc. Start going to school from tomorrow. May God bless you!" Having said so, the mistress embraced him and wiped his tears. Then she gave him some money as a reward for his honesty.

Having heard the mistress's sympathetic words, the boy's heart leapt up with joy. He expressed his gratitude to her. He started going to school and as a result of his hard work and truth, he became a talented scholar and a well reputed person.

Truth of a Small Boy

Two small boys were going along a road. On their way, in a garden, multi-coloured flowers were blooming. That area was full of the fragrance of flowers. Having seen the flowers, one of the boys said, "If I had got a few flowers, I would have given to my sick sister and she would have been much pleased." Having heard this, the second boy said, "Then why don't you pluck flowers? If being small, you are unable to pluck, I may pluck for you, because I am taller than you." The first boy said to him, "No, it is not proper and justified. Plucking flowers without permission is a theft, which is an evil. I'll request the owner to give me a few flowers." But the second boy plucked a bunch of flowers. The gardener saw him plucking the bunch of flowers from a distance, caught him, beat him and kept him as a prisoner.

Then the first boy knocked at the door. From inside, an old, kind woman opened the gate. The boy said, "Dear mother, will you kindly give me one or two roses for my sick sister?"

The old woman said, "Very happily, dear son. I was listening to the conversation which was going on between you and the other boy. You are a very good boy. Come with me, I'll pluck you a bunch of beautiful roses."

The old woman plucked the bunch and said to him, "Whenever your sister demands flowers, come here and take flowers for her." Not only this, the old woman went to meet that boy's sick sister and mother and gave expenses for the education of that boy. When he had completed his education, that woman gave him an employment. Thus truth always bears good fruit.

An Honest Poor Boy

There was a poor boy. In his family there were two other members—his mother and his younger sister. His sister was ill. He was going to his uncle to inform him that his sister needed the doctor's treatment. On the way he found a purse containing One hundred and twenty rupees.

The boy was very honest. He determined that he would discover the owner of the purse and would hand over his purse to him. He told this incident to his mother and said, "Mother! The gentleman, who lost this purse, must be worried because it contains money. If we have this money, we'll incur a deadly sin and God will be displeased with us. But the problem is how to find out the owner of this money. Please tell me how I should discover him."

His mother was also very honest. Having listened to her son, she was very much pleased. She said, "My son! May God make your resolve firm and may you be blessed! If the news is published in a newspaper, the owner of the money will come and take his purse back."

The boy went to a printing press where the newspaper was published. The owner of the newspaper published the news, seeing the honesty of the boy. The advertisement was—'I found a purse containing one hundred and twenty rupees. The owner is requested to take the money by coming to such and such place, after giving proof." Having read the advertisement, the owner of the purse came there and he was wonderstruck to see that the boy, in spite of his poverty, was honest.

The owner of the purse said "He who, in spite of being poor, is not tempted to be greedy for money, is really honest and praiseworthy. In fact only poor people are so honest. The rich people, in spite of having enough money, out of greed for money, become dishonest. You are blessed that you, having faith in God, remained firm in your resolve of truth." Having said so, that gentleman gave that money insistingly to the boy for the medical treatment and medicines for his younger sister and employed the boy under him. The boy in future, because of his honesty, became a reputed and rich businessman.

An Honest Boy, the Son to the Hotel-Owner

A businessman was going to a foreign country. On his way at night he stayed in a hotel and the next morning he went away from there. Having reached his destination, he saw that his purse was missing. It contained three hundred rupees. The businessman lost hope to get his purse back and he forgot this incident.

When the businessman had gone away, the boy, who was the son to the hotel owner, saw the purse lying in the courtyard of the hotel. He instead of touching it, went straight way to his father and conveyed this message. The father said to him, "Put some leaves and branches of the tree on the purse and cover it." So the son covered it with leaves and branches.

After some days the same businessman, while returning, stayed in the same hotel at night. While he was talking to the owner of the hotel, he mentioned that he had lost his purse. Having listened to him, the owner, the father of the boy, who had found the purse, said to the businessman. "Please, go with my son. He will show you your purse. He has not even touched it. He has just covered it with leaves and branches."

That businessman went with the boy and he, having removed the leaves and branches, took out his purse. He praised the boy very much.

Thus such a boy, who does not want even to touch the money of others, is considered very honest.

Truthfulness of the Vegetable-seller Boy

In market, a boy was selling vegetables and there was an another boy also, who also sold vegetables. One day a man came to the shop of the farmer boy, and taking a water-melon in his hand, asked the boy, "Is it fresh and good?" The boy said, "Sir, it seems fresh and good but actually it is rotten and insipid." The gentleman, while leaving his shop, said to the boy, "You are honest, so your sales will be down."

The boy said, "I'll speak the truth. If the customer wants to buy, he will buy, otherwise he will not. I'll not tell a lie." The gentleman then went to the neighbouring shop and he asked the boy, "O boy! Is this cucumber fresh?" The boy replied, "Yes, Sir, it is fresh." That gentleman bought the cucumber and went home. When the gentleman had gone, this boy said to the other vegetable-seller boy. "You are a fool. You should have not spoken the truth. I told a lie and sold my stale cucumber by declaring it fresh. Now you will have to throw your water-melon as rubbish."

Hearing this, the honest boy said, "I'll never tell a lie. I don't mind whether my vegetables are sold or not. I speak the truth and this truth provides me peace and finally

God gives a reward for truth."

When the gentleman ate the cucumber, he knew that the boy had cheated him. So from the next day he began to buy vegetables and fruits from the shop of the honest boy. He never brought anything from the shop of the dishonest boy. By and by the citizens came to know the honesty of the honest boy and most of the customers came to him to buy vegetables and fruits. So he had a roaring trade, while his neighbouring dishonest boy remained poor.

Truthfulness of a Boy-Scout

Once in a school, students were solving their Mathematics question paper in the examination hall. The paper was tough and so students were unable to solve all the questions. A boy somehow managed to send the question paper out of the hall to his friend, who sent back the solution of all the questions. All the students copied the answers in their answer books. Out of those students, there was a boy-scout. First he hesitated to copy the answers but finally he adopted this foul means in order to pass the examination. When the time was over, he handed over his answer book to the invigilator and went home.

In the evening before going to bed, as per rule, he read the rules which a boy-scout should obey. Having read the first rule, he became restless. According to the rule, he had to speak the truth but that day he had done something contrary to the truth. He repented of his sin very much. Immediately he put on his clothes, went to the house of his headmaster and knocked at his door. The headmaster asked him why he had come there. He narrated the whole incident truly and said, "I have committed a deadly sin. Kindly punish me for my sin whatever you deem fit."

The headmaster said, "You have already been punished. You will be re-examined in Mathematics."

That boy was re-examined in Mathematics and he passed, securing good marks. Other students, who had copied, were punished.